Working
in sport

Visit our How To website at www.howto.co.uk

At www.howto.co.uk you can en██████conversation with our authors – all of whom have 'been████e and done that' in their specialist fields. You can get access to special offers and additional content but most importantly you will be able to engage with, and become a part of, a wide and growing community of people just like yourself.

At www.howto.co.uk you'll be able to talk and share tips with people who have similar interests and are facing similar challenges in their lives. People who, just like you, have the desire to change their lives for the better – be it through moving to a new country, starting a new business, growing their own vegetables, or writing a novel.

At www.howto.co.uk you'll find the support and encouragement you need to help make your aspirations a reality.

How To Books strives to present authentic, inspiring, practical information in their books. Now, when you buy a title from **How To Books,** you get even more than just words on a page.

Working in sport

How to find a sports related job in the UK or abroad

James Masters

WISE LRC
FILTON COLLEGE
NEW ROAD
STOKE GIFFORD
BRISTOL
BS34 8LP

howtobooks

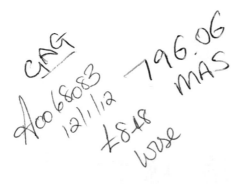

Published by How To Books Ltd,
Spring Hill House, Spring Hill Road,
Begbroke, Oxford OX5 1RX, United Kingdom
Tel: (01865) 375794. Fax: (01865) 379162
info@howtobooks.co.uk
www.howtobooks.co.uk

British Library Cataloguing in Publication Data
A catalogue record for this book is available from the British Library

ISBN: 978 1 84528 455 8

First edition 1999
Second edition 2007
Third edition 2011

Cover design by Baseline Arts Ltd, Oxford
Produced for How To Books by Deer Park Productions, Tavistock, Devon
Typeset by PDQ Typesetting Ltd, Staffordshire
Printed and bound in Great Britain by Bell & Bain Ltd, Glasgow

NOTE: The material contained in this book is set out in good faith for general guidance
and no liability can be accepted for loss or expense incurred as a result of relying in
particular circumstances on statements made in the book. Laws and regulations are
complex and liable to change, and readers should check the current position with the
relevant authorities before making personal arrangements.

Contents

List of Illustrations

Foreword

I first met James in the summer of 1990 and he was my mentor until the Sydney Paralympics in 2000, where his coaching helped me achieve my second Paralympic Javelin Gold medal under his guidance (I had already won in Atlanta 1996). I had also become the World Champion in both Berlin in 1994 and Birmingham 1998 as well as breaking the world record on several occasions.

No small part of my achievements was due to James's input. He really is an outstanding coach, and I believe that the advice that he gives to his athletes and similarly in this book, are of an equally high standard.

James has helped a multitude of people gain employment in sport, not only in this country but all over the world as well. I know that it was after advising his own group of athletes, basketball players and students on the opportunities that exist in sports employment that he realised that youngsters throughout the country would also benefit from this knowledge. So he wrote the first edition of *Working in Sport*.

This in now the third edition of the book. I'm sure that the first two have helped hundreds of people get sports-related employment and as this is the best one yet (he says), then obviously this one will be just as invaluable to loads more people. I hope that you are one of them and that you get the job that you are looking for.

Ken Churchill

Preface

This is the third edition of this book, and although the previous two have been well received and critically acclaimed, I am more excited about this one. Not only is it the most comprehensive book yet, but it is the London Olympics version and that makes it very special.

The Olympic Games were last held Britain in 1948, so it is unlikely that they will be held here again in the next 50 years. That makes this book unique, as another opportunity such as this is unlikely to come round again (unless I'm still writing at over 100 years old) to produce a book of this nature.

London 2012 is an enormous undertaking for the organising committee, LOCOG, and as a result a multitude of jobs have been created in order to bring this Olympiad to fruition. Workers are needed before, during and after the Games, with the aim of making them the best and most memorable yet. It doesn't end there either. Many of the jobs are permanent, and will endure long after the memory of the Games has faded.

So many jobs have been created that the normal format of the book has been extended by an extra chapter, in order to adequately cover the wealth of new opportunities that are now out there.

The explosion of broadband availability, and the number of homes with computer access, have totally revolutionised the direction that this third edition takes. When the first edition was printed, broadband was almost unheard of in the UK. Many businesses and schools had it, but only rich private individuals could afford it at home. Even the computer that I am now using at £450 is more powerful than the one I used in those days, which cost nearly ten times as much.

The first edition mainly focused on providing information with references to other books and magazines; very few web addresses were given. The second edition evolved into providing far more internet references, whereas this version relies heavily on the world wide web.

Normal 'snail mail' contact addresses and telephone numbers are still provided, as many people still prefer books as their main source of reference, or indeed, might not have the use of a computer. Please excuse, however, the fact that the book is biased towards the internet and if you do have difficulty in contacting the person or company that you require, don't be afraid of asking at your local library for help. Most libraries in the UK now provide free internet access (normally for one hour) and the librarians are usually only too happy to assist you in navigating your way around the computer.

Good luck with finding your dream job – I hope that it comes as a result of reading this book.

ACKNOWLEDGEMENTS

As in the previous edition it would not have been possible to write this book without the invaluable assistance of the people listed below. If I have missed anybody from this list, I apologise, it wasn't intentional.

The following people and organisations have given invaluable assistance in compiling this book. My sincere thanks go to them, as without their help this book would be far less interesting.

Steven Armstrong, Steve Atkinson, Gareth Couzens, Jim Eason, Karen Flint, Simon Flint, Kath Gratton, Ollie Haum, Ian Jefferson, John Little, Mike Latcham, Ian McGuckin, Simon Mitchell, plus Andy Bell of *Soccer Coach*, USA, Stuart Dowsett of *Brussels Barbarians RFC*, John Gaylard and *Horse & Hound* magazine, David Holmes at *British Dressage*, Martin Hudson at *P.G.L.*, *Mark Warner Ltd*, *Rugby World* magazine, Dave Sturdy and *Four Four Two* magazine, David Wear at *Beamish Open Air Museum* and last alphabetically, but not least, Tim Woodhouse from the *Women's Sport and Fitness Foundation*.

Although every effort has been made to ensure that this book is as accurate and up to date as is possible, no liability can be accepted by the author or publisher. Things change. It is inevitable that during the lifetime of this book some of the data will become outdated and some errors or omissions will become evident. Readers should satisfy themselves as to the book's accuracy before relying on it. No liability can be accepted by the author or publisher for disappointment, loss, negligence or other damage caused by relying solely on the information that this book contains, nor in the event of bankruptcy, liquidation or cessation of trade of any company, individual or firm.

James Masters

1

Making the Most of Your Skills

Like most teenagers I had no idea what career I was going to pursue when I left school. Foolishly, attracted by the salary, I chose accountancy as my profession, but this didn't sit easy with my loud and hyperactive personality. So, after a very short period of employment, I returned to sixth-form college. Even more fortunately, one of my tutors dissuaded me from my next choice of career when she revealed that she thought that I had natural ability as a teacher. So, luckily, I abandoned the idea of joining the armed forces. Otherwise I could now be sitting in a war zone in Afghanistan.

Experiences such as the above are not rare. Teenagers, as well as many adults, often make poor, initial career choices. This should not happen. Making a life-changing decision when you are barely out of nappies is not, logically, a wise move. You need to be experienced or well-informed – two things that normally come with age.

This is one of the major reasons why this book has been written. The career advice I received at my school was terrible, and although things have greatly improved since then, there are still far too many people ending up in employment that is totally wrong for them. It is intended that readers of this book will be guided by it and not just drift into any old job that comes along, as many of us do.

I was fortunate that I was academically minded (*not much*), but enough, to get through college and qualify as a teacher. Academic qualifications are not, however, an absolute necessity. You don't need to possess masses of paper certificates to land your dream job. Many other qualities and skills contribute too.

It *is* true, though, that the more skills and qualifications that you have to impress an employer, academic or not, then the more chance you have of achieving your desired career. This will be dealt with in more detail in Chapter 7.

In the meantime, don't just drift with the wind, and settle for any job that comes along. That is a sure-fire way of ending up in employment that you are not happy with. If there is a particular career that you would love to pursue, don't immediately write it off as being unachievable, but research it. The internet is a great place to start. Find out what qualifications or skills you need, and then realistically assess your chances of acquiring these. You may then decide that this dream is not achievable but your research will probably unearth a multitude of other jobs within that sector that you had not considered, and might have the ability to achieve.

However, you have to be realistic.

Most youngsters dream about one day being rich and famous. Some dream about being a film star or a successful pop singer. For others the fantasy is of scoring the winning goal at Wembley, or taking the trophy at Wimbledon or the US Masters. Unfortunately this is normally as far as it gets, because only one person in the whole world each year can achieve this dream out of the millions, *literally* millions, who have dreamt it.

PURSUING YOUR DREAM

That doesn't mean, however, that it is not worth trying to pursue your fantasy. Somebody has got to achieve it, but you cannot live life in a dream world. A lot of reality has got to be mixed with a little fantasy. You have got to be *exceptionally* talented, with nerves of steel and a will to work extremely hard to get that far. Most people lack at least one of the necessary qualities. Even the people who possess all of them still find themselves in an incredibly large pool of very talented people.

Fortunately, though, this doesn't have to be the end of your sporting dream. There are still numerous other opportunities, besides being a pro sportsman, that would enable you to make a career out of your sport, or at least to simply enjoy it while it lasts.

In the first edition of this book I reported that the Central Council for Physical Recreation (CCPR)[1] estimated there to be nearly half a million people making their living out of working in sport in Britain. This number has now risen dramatically.

In 2005 it was estimated that 40,000 people worked in sport in Scotland alone. The leisure industry continues to be a huge growth area for the employment of British citizens at home and an increasing number working abroad. If you add the number of these foreign workers to our national employment figures then the amount of Brits working in some form of sporting capacity is now astronomical.

Mark Warner Ltd is one of the leaders in the provision of 'active' holidays in Britain. Each year they employ over 1,500 staff to work in some of Europe's top ski resorts and locations around the Mediterranean and Aegean, and there are many other big employers in this field including Club Med, Crystal Holidays, First Choice, PGL, etc., all of whose contact information can be found in Chapter 10.

There are sports-related jobs out there for all standards of playing and coaching ability, as well as all levels of academic achievement. If you are determined enough, with the ability to match, you too could be working in sport, *soon*.

MAKING THE RIGHT MOVE

Would you enjoy it?
Working in sport and enjoying playing it are not one and the same. You often have to work long, unsociable hours coaching other people to compete in the sport that you love. Worse still, you could spend all day cleaning and preparing the equipment or playing area for others to use. Would you enjoy it?

Are you ready and qualified for it?
Don't forget that many other people also want to work in sport. Hundreds of applications are regularly received by employers for these jobs, especially in our bigger cities. To increase your chances of success you may need to move away from home or take extra academic qualifications. Are you prepared to do this?

If you can answer yes to either of the above questions, and have not been put off by the realities of the situation, then maybe this *is* the right move for you. However, if you think that you can just walk into the ideal job straight after leaving school or college, you are most likely to join the long list of disappointed dreamers.

ASSESSING WHETHER THIS MOVE IS RIGHT FOR YOU
1. Examine the flowchart in Figure 1.

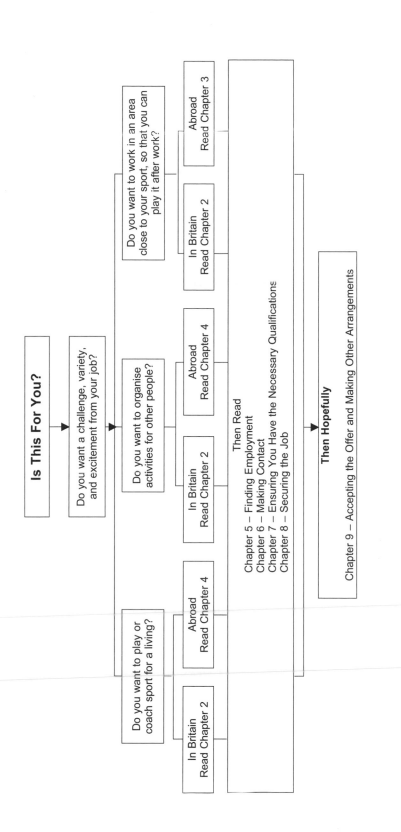

Fig. 1. Self-assessment flowchart.

2. Find the category in which you would like to find employment.

3. Read the relevant sections in the chapters indicated.

If you are still determined to work in sport, in whatever capacity, it is worth weighing up the pros and cons of this option in Figure 2.

PROS	CONS
◆ Varied workload.	◆ Not a steady 9 to 5 job.
◆ Healthy lifestyle.	◆ Will probably have to work much harder than in an office.
◆ Not boring and repetitive.	◆ May have to work long and irregular hours.
◆ Often gives opportunities to travel.	◆ May have to be away from home frequently.
◆ On site to compete at your own sport.	◆ Often too tired to compete after work.
◆ You get to meet many interesting people.	◆ You may also have to work with people that you don't like.
◆ Satisfaction from achieving something worthwhile.	◆ Often under pressure to resolve tricky situations.
◆ On site to train for your own sport.	◆ After working all day at this site, you may not feel motivated to train there.

Fig. 2. Weighing up the pros and cons.

Still undeterred? Then the following suggestions will help you in your quest.

IMPROVING YOUR CHANCES

Chapter 7, 'Ensuring You Have the Necessary Qualifications', will tell you what employers require from you. Many jobs need some sort of formal qualifications, so if you don't have the necessary certificates and diplomas you have three choices:

1. Set about acquiring them.

2. Look for a job more suited to your ability.

3. Still apply, hoping that you have other qualities they might be looking for.

Whatever your level of academic qualifications, you can still improve your chances by acquiring some easily obtained skills and experience. These should always be included in your CV or on the application form when applying for work. For example:

- aptitude for car maintenance;
- coaching awards;
- computer literacy;
- council self-help scheme;
- DIY ability;
- driving licence;
- first aid certificate;
- language skills;
- life-saving awards;
- musical ability;
- part-time work;
- sports certificates, awards and trophies;
- scouting;

- typing certificates or expertise;
- voluntary work;
- working for a charity, a youth club, or in a crèche.

I am sure there are many others that haven't been thought of, so don't forget, always include any experience you have gained that you think is relevant to the job for which you are applying. All inclusions will improve your profile and might just give you the edge in interviews. If you don't find the more academic qualifications particularly easy you can still impress prospective employers by gaining some practical qualifications and experience. Adverts for these, and many other courses, regularly appear in your local newspapers. Alternatively you can pop down to your local community college for a prospectus of their courses, as many of these will be based there, and if not they will probably point you in the direction of the course you are looking for.

The basic level certificate is normally quite easy to achieve and within everyone's reach.

Thinking of everything

When applying for a job make sure that you put all of your skills down on your application form. For example, if the work that you are applying for is in England it might not seem relevant to tell the employer that you speak Japanese. However, that company might have a group of Japanese businessmen visiting them during the summer and your ability to communicate with them might give you the edge over other applicants.

An ability to use a computer is always worth mentioning, even if you can do little more than type letters on it. It shows that you are not scared of using one, and that you are likely to be easily trained to do more than you are presently capable of.

Likewise if you are skilful at woodwork, metalwork, needlecraft or other practical skills, mention them. They could be something that the employer is looking for, or could be an indication of your ability to learn another skill. Don't forget that employers don't generally expect you just to start work immediately with all the required skills in place, and will invariably train you up to the standard they require.

Gaining experience

If you don't have any certificates or skills there are other things that impress employers and you mustn't be shy of using them. 'The University of Life' often gives you the *experience* that companies are looking for and many employers place as much importance on this as on the qualifications you might also have gained.

Simply asking at the local hospital or charity if you could do some voluntary work will often lead to a very impressive inclusion in your CV. Libraries are a good source of information if you need to find out about these. *Yellow Pages* can also be useful. Well over 100 different addresses and telephone numbers of various charities are contained in most directories.

Don't forget that working for somebody is only part of the advantage to you. Not only do you gain the experience of the employment to put on your CV, but also, if you have done well at this job, you should get a valuable reference from your employer

Being given references

Strictly speaking a reference is written confidentially and sent privately to your prospective employer. If you are personally given a written citation from your employer it is called a testimonial. However, over the years these terms seem to have been confused, so it is worth checking which of the two is required by the company to which you are applying.

The following points regarding references and testimonials should be observed.

◆ Any references supplied to the employer should be suitable for the job. A reference regarding your experience and expertise as a joiner might be of little value if you are applying to be a bus driver, unless it mentions your employability, punctuality, reliability and honesty.

◆ If you haven't had a previous job then a reference or testimonial from your head teacher or principal, schoolteacher, Scout leader, vicar or even a friend could be supplied. They *must* emphasise the strong points of your character.

◆ *All* references and testimonials should be typed, on suitably headed paper. Something scribbled on a scrap of paper not only reflects poorly on you, but could also make the employer suspect that it is a forgery.

◆ *Any* references and testimonials are as valuable to you as academic qualifications. In both cases, keep them safe and in good condition. You will probably use them over and over again. If they look scruffy your interviewer will probably suspect that your standard of work will also lack care and attention.

SELF-ASSESSMENT EXERCISE

1. Is employment in sport right for you? Can you cope with the disadvantages *as well as* the advantages? Remember it is not a regular nine to five job.

2. Are you fit enough to cope with the workload? Don't forget that it will be physically more demanding than sitting behind a desk and the hours may be longer.

3. As this type of work is much sought after you may not be able to get a job close to home. Are you prepared to move anywhere in Britain or abroad?

4. Are you resilient enough to deal with awkward and obnoxious people? Don't forget that working in sport is a 'people' thing.

5. Can you work under pressure? You might sometimes be required to work late to finish a project and also work to a tight deadline.

6. Would you prefer to work abroad? Do you know which country you prefer? Do you know anything about the country? Are you prepared to learn the language?

7. Has the work got to be on a long-term contract? Do you mind temporary work?

8. Have you got the necessary experience and qualifications for this job and, if not, are you prepared to work to get them?

2
Discovering the Opportunities in Britain

PLAYING THE GAME

When you are younger it is quite natural to wonder what you will do when you leave school. It is not normal, however, to dream of becoming a greenkeeper, or a sports centre manager or even a coach in your favourite sport. The fantasy is nearly always of playing for your local professional team, or if even more ambitious of representing Great Britain at a World Cup or Olympic Games.

Most children would play for their local team just for the love of it, regardless of the prestige, the adoration of the fans and the excitement. Money would not be an issue.

A spin-off, though, could be that by fulfilling their dreams they might also have carved out a very lucrative career.

Playing for gold

The kind of money that top soccer players earn is well documented. Recently David Beckham was reported in 2009 to have been paid an annual salary of $5.5 million by L.A. Galaxy, but this figure was more than doubled with his cut of the team's sponsorship, ticket and merchandise revenue. Then, add to this his own personal advertising deals with Adidas, Pepsi and Motorola and his total annual income amounts to approximately £31 million GBP.

Unfortunately, though, not all sports have competitors who earn as much as professional footballers, *but some earn even more.*

Over the year of 2009, the top earner worldwide was reputedly Tiger Woods, but it must be noted that none of this was salaried income. In other words, unlike Beckham, he didn't have a guaranteed income to fall back on if his tournament winnings and sponsorship deals dried up. His reported earnings for 2009 were estimated to be a staggering £30 million. Unfortunately, as predicted, his earnings for 2010 are considered to have fallen dramatically due to the withdrawal of his sponsorship and absence from tournaments due to the scandal created after the revelations of his extramarital affairs.

Every year the *Sunday Times* produces its 'Rich List',[2] which estimates the total wealth of the richest people in Britain. It is staggering to note that for 2010 the total fortune of the richest sportsman, David Beckham, combined with the millions earned by his wife, Victoria, through music and fashion, doesn't even place them in the top 400.

All the places above him are filled by people who have made their fortune in industry, retail and property. So if your intention is merely to become extremely wealthy, maybe this is where you should set your sights.

The super-rich, above the Beckhams, that have sporting connections, all made their money first before becoming well known for their involvement with sport. For example, the second richest person on the list is the owner of Chelsea Football Club, Roman Abramovich, who made his vast £7,400 millions through oil and other industries.

Bernie Ecclestone, who is 38th on the list and reputedly worth £1,375 million, did however start as a competitor – not a good one – but made his fortune through managing and administrating Formula One racing.

Mike Ashley, the controversial owner of Newcastle United FC, was very rich (£890m), before joining them. He made his money through owning a chain of sports goods stores, as did David Bromilow (94th; and worth £650m) and Dave Whelan (336th and £190m).

Sir John Madejski (Chairman of Reading FC) amassed his £200m wealth mainly through publishing *Auto Trader*.

A notable non-sports, personality above the Beckhams is Simon Cowell (£165m), who made his fortune through music and TV, although David and Victoria *are* worth more than Ringo Starr and Tim Rice, who are both worth £140m and Tom Jones (£135m).

The other sportsmen who made the top 2000 of the *Sunday Times* list did not necessarily make their fortune solely through their sporting prowess. Most of them added to their wages through TV appearances, advertising deals and shrewd investments, amongst other sources of income.

One of the surprises on the list, for example, Robbie Fowler, generated much of his £31m through his property business, as well as football.

It may appear that the wealthiest people in sport are all soccer players, but this is not true: after the Beckhams comes a variety of other athletes. Boxer Lennox Lewis is reported to be worth

£95m, and Jody Scheckter, the ex-F1 driver, made his wealth (£60m) through sport and running self-defence schools.

The next two sportsmen on the list were also involved with Formula One racing. David Coulthard is reputedly worth £50m and Jenson Button £43m.

Football then dominates the list, with the joint wealth of Wayne and Colleen Rooney showing at 1522nd with £41 million.

Michael Owen (£40m), Alan Shearer (£33m), Rio Ferdinand (£33m), Sol Campbell (£33m) and Ryan Giggs (£32m) are also prominent on the list before golfer Nick Faldo appears with £32m.

The only other sportsman who breaks that run of footballers is another F1 driver Lewis Hamilton, who ranks 1719th with £35 million. The surprise in this list, and I believe the only football manager ever to be ranked in the top 2000, was Fabio Capello, England manager, whose reputed £34m wealth ranked him 1776th.

What I also find incredible about the *Sunday Times* Rich List 2010 is that we have just emerged from one of the worst recessions and banking crises in history and yet the lowest earner, with sporting connections, was Barry Hearn (promoter) ranked 1905th with a meagre £30m, whereas just four years ago, when the second edition of this book was published, it was Luke Donald (golf) with £25 million less.

So you can see, although it may be just a dream and highly unlikely that you will make it to the top of the tree, if your dream does come true, there is the potential to be a huge earner, whatever your sport.

Football riches

As you can see from the above list, in Britain, the average footballer earns more money than other sportsmen. However, on a worldwide scale other sportsmen earn much more. The top five American Footballers (that is 'gridiron' as opposed to 'soccer') for the 2009/10 season were paid a basic wage (i.e. not including endorsements) of $20.32 million (£12.8m) whereas the top 5 soccer players in the world made $14.67 million (£9.24m). David Beckham's salary paled into insignificance when compared with Portugal's Christiano Ronaldo's $17.06m from Real Madrid.

The second-highest paid footballer was Sweden's Zlatan Ibrahimovic, who earned a reported $15.7 million whilst playing for Barcelona. Third was Argentinian Lionel Messi, also with Barcelona, whose contract was worth $13.74m. Fourth was the captain of Cameroon's national team, Samuel Eto'o, who was paid $13.74 million by Italy's Internazionale club, and fifth was Brazilian Ricardo Izecson dos Santos Leite (more commonly known as Kaka to fans), who made $13.13 million while also playing for Real Madrid.

The first English Premiership players to appear in the top 20 on this list were: in equal 8th spot, John Terry and Frank Lampard both of Chelsea, and Steven Gerrard of Liverpool, who all earned $9.81m. 15th was the German, Michael Ballack, again of Chelsea, who earned $8.45 million. 17th was Rio Ferdinand of Manchester United who took home $8.45 million. 18th, Kolo Toure (Ivory Coast), earning $8.45 million from Manchester City. 19th, Wayne Rooney, also Manchester United ($7.85 million). 20th the Brazilian Robinho of Manchester City, who earned $7.85 million.

(source: Kaitlin Madden, CareerBuilder.com and Futebol Finance[3])

These, remember, are the *top* paid players in the world, but what can the 'normal' person earn who has chosen football as his preferred profession? Although footballer's pay is notoriously hard to pin down, we can only make a shrewd educated estimate based on the most recent survey that was conducted by the PFA (Professional Footballers' Association).[4] In 2006 they calculated that wages had risen by an average of approximately 11% since 2000, so, if we then use this yardstick to gauge the rise in wages since 2006, it is reasonable to assume that, even taken into account the recent recession, and the *Sunday Times* Rich List, that wages will have risen *at least* 30% in the last four years. Therefore Premiership footballers who in 2006 earned an average of £676,000 per annum should now be earning approximately £879,000 using the above guidelines.

Likewise, Championship players should earn an approximate average of £255,000, League One players should earn around about £88,000 on average, with League Two footballers on an average of £64,500.

Competing with foreign players

Unfortunately, though, it is becoming increasingly difficult for British players to achieve the top wages in football as the Premiership is flooded with more and more foreign players. Last season both Chelsea and Arsenal, on more than one occasion, turned out teams containing only a couple of British players. Even their managers are imports.

This situation is by no means unusual. The *Times* also reported in their most recent survey that 187 foreigners from 50 different countries played in the Premiership.

This may be good for the standard of the game, but it leaves fewer jobs to go round for our home grown talent. It is also

becoming increasingly hard to gain a place in our lower division teams, with more and more foreign nationals playing there. Even some of our second division teams now boast Brazilian and Argentinian players.

Going abroad or staying in the UK

This means that many of our own better players need to move abroad to increase their earning potential.

Due to the influx of foreign players in our game, many of our top footballers who don't go abroad are relegated to being substitutes, playing in the reserves or even in the lower divisions.

Nevertheless, as shown above, a decent living wage can still be earned. Even semi-professional players in the Conference or Northern League can earn more than £200 per week and, of course, this can be topped up by money earned through their other sidelines.

Getting into soccer

Getting into paid employment in soccer is not easy though. The Professional Footballers' Association has approximately 4,000 members, and although this figure seems quite high, it is absolutely tiny in comparison with the number of 'applicants' rejected. The failure rate in football is exceptionally high.

Almost every player gets into football by being discovered, rather than applying. Usually they are spotted whilst playing for a minor team and then approached by a scout or someone from the management team of a bigger and wealthier club. If the player they are interested in is still at school they will approach the parents or head teacher. If the player is older they will be approached through their club and invited to attend either a trial or training sessions, where they can be assessed.

Some players *have* written to non-Football League clubs, been offered trials and later been taken on as semi-professionals, but this is rare.

PLAYING OTHER SPORTS

We must remember, though, that football is not the only professional sport in Britain. The Rich List quoted above contained high earners from boxing, motor racing and golf. Wealthy sportspeople can also be found in athletics, snooker, darts, horse racing, tennis and rugby.

In recent years many of the more traditionally amateur sports have become 'open', resulting in more professional playing opportunities than ever before. Some of these sports are detailed below.

Rugby Union

Rugby Union has been a professional sport since 1995. (Rugby League turned pro a long time before this.)

Just as with soccer, rugby clubs in Britain are now swamped with foreign players, making less opportunities for British players to earn a living here. It is estimated that there are now more than 2000 full-time professionals playing in the Guinness Premiership.[5] The top earner is Carl Hayman, a prop from New Zealand, who earns £370,000 a year. The highest paid player in the world is Sebastian Chabal (Paris Racing Metro) on a reported $1.8 million. The top players worldwide, similar to footballers, receive these wages plus lucrative sponsorship deals and other earnings.

The top Rugby Union players' salaries in the UK are on average between £150k and £300k p.a., but home-grown players normally earn between £40,000 and £75,000 a year, with full-time senior (18 +) Academy players earning approximately £25k p.a.

The big money in Rugby Union, worldwide, is being paid in the Six Nations Championship countries, with France and Britain being the highest payers. This is why so many Australian, South African, South Sea Island and New Zealand players are plying their trade here rather than in the Southern Hemisphere.

However, British players are still in big demand abroad, and even players of lesser ability can still find clubs to play for in the developing rugby nations, although whether a living wage would be available here is debatable. Many foreign clubs offer 'packages' which generally means assistance with finding employment and a place to live, sometimes travel expenses and/or a small playing fee might be included. It all really depends on how big a club you are joining, and how good a player you are.

Finding opportunities

Rugby World was always the magazine to find adverts for 'players wanted'. It is still useful in this respect, but now several websites are springing up on the internet that also offer further opportunities to aspiring professionals. Rugbyrecruit.com and rugbyrugby.com are just two of these. The latter, for example, recently contained these two adverts:

Rugby La Vila
Spanish Premiership Club based in Benidorm.
Looking for a number 3 with Spanish Passport.
Professional offer. August to March inclusive.

Chicago USA
Top Club looking for players for the Fall,
Props and Locks needed but all positions considered.
Travel expenses, work, and housing for right player.

The traffic, however, goes both ways, in previous seasons both Reading and Stockton RFC were asking their members if they could find employment for four young Australians and New Zealanders who wanted to play in Britain.

Athletics

Few athletes make a living out of their sport. Even at British League level the majority competing in the first division receive little more than hotel and travel expenses for their efforts. Some receive a little extra through grants and personal sponsorship, but this is rarely enough to live on. It is only the really talented few who make it onto the Grand Prix circuit who can afford to live comfortably. They then get appearance money, prize money if they are good enough and possibly television royalties.

Generally, money isn't available to pay other athletes. The sport doesn't attract enough paying spectators or television coverage to generate enough income, even from international matches.

It is estimated, however, that more than 300 athletes do make enough money out of their sport to live on. Most of this money comes from being a household name such as Colin Jackson and Steve Cram, and is boosted by regular TV appearances, radio and newspaper interviews, after dinner speeches and personal sponsorship. Linford Christie and Daley Thompson reputedly made more than £1 million in this fashion, so current personalities should expect to accumulate more than this.

For the less fortunate, National Lottery funding is still given to those who are considered medal prospects at the major championships or to those developing athletes who are considered future prospects.

A precarious living

Although all of the above sounds very promising, to put it in perspective 300 athletes out of literally thousands who join local athletics clubs is not a great proportion. Plus, don't forget, the opportunities to earn only stretch over approximately four months of the outdoor season and a very short indoor season. Athletes then have to fund more than six months of out of season training. An athlete also reduces their earning potential if they are injured, and if the injury is major or for a long duration they could also lose their sponsorship, training grant and also miss out on prize money and advertising. Very precarious!

TURNING PROFESSIONAL

You have to be really outstanding at your sport if you are to earn money from it. Many sports don't have a wage structure as such, because the competitors make their money by tournament earnings, appearance money and exhibition matches. In these cases it is even more vital to be better than the next person because inferior performances mean an inferior standard of living.

Attendance at the next tournament often incurs travel expenses and hotel bills, so it is probably no surprise to learn that the majority of professionals either scrape a meagre existence from their sport, or are forced into part-time employment, fitting their training and competitions around this. Some are forced to play as an amateur in order to obtain a regular wage, often from non-sports related employment. Ironically, some amateurs make more money through their sport than they would do as a lower level professional.

Being a semi-pro

Unfortunately most sports careers are short, the average being between seven and ten years of full-time employment, depending on the type of sport you play. Contact sports are often at the lower end of career span. As a result most professional clubs encourage their players to improve their qualifications and experience in order to gain employment when their playing career ends. The semi-pro often has an advantage over their full-time counterpart in this respect, because they already have experience of other work and possibly another career to fall back on.

EARNING THROUGH COMPETING

Details of sports from which you can make enough money to live on would fill a book like this. Listed below are just some of them. If your sport is not included here it does not mean that it is not possible to make a living from it, but the best way to find out if this is possible is to contact your national organising body. The more popular of these are listed in Chapter 6.

If you would like more specific information about these sports, look in the appropriate publications in the book information section of Chapter 10.

angling	ice hockey	soccer
athletics (track and field)	judo	speedway
badminton	karting	squash
basketball	motor racing	surfing
bmx	mountain biking	swimming
boxing	power boating	table tennis
cricket	rally driving	ten pin bowling
cycling	rugby league	tennis
darts	rugby union	volleyball
equestrianism	skiing	waterskiing
golf	snooker	windsurfing
horse racing		

It is vital to stress again that not all (or even many) of the sports on this list are wage-earning. Most depend on players performing well in tournaments and accumulating prize money, or receiving appearance money. Of course this can also be boosted by advertising, sponsorship, television appearance and exhibition fees.

Sponsorship

Sports like canoeing, where professionals survive merely on sponsorship that they themselves or their association raise, are not included in the list. It would be unfair to include these as the world of sponsorship is extremely fickle. Companies often withdraw sponsorship when there is a downturn in the economic climate, as has recently occurred, leaving many recipients high and dry. (No pun intended!)

Sponsorship is, however, the backbone of British sport. Most sports rely on it, to varying degrees, to provide an existence for their professional competitors that would otherwise be impossible. There can be no doubt that without sponsorship there would be far fewer professional sportspeople.

A number of professionals also supplement their earnings by giving demonstrations and holding coaching clinics, snooker is a good example of this, but if you compete regularly you have limited time to give to such work.

Going abroad

There are also several sports in which competitors find it difficult to earn a living in Britain, but by moving abroad may be able to do so. Cycling, powerboating, judo, skateboarding, snowboarding, swimming, squash, surfing and windsurfing are amongst these. Volleyball is typical of them all; we have several British players competing in clubs in Belgium, France and

Switzerland because they can't make enough money out of their sport in their own country.

Golf pros

Being a professional takes on another meaning, however, in golf more than in other sports. Here, if you make money through playing you are called a tournament professional, whereas if you make your living through instructing, organising tournaments and running the golf shop, you would be called a club pro. If you are interested in becoming either of these you need to contact the PGA whose details are in Chapter 6.

WOMEN IN SPORT

Competing

In the previous edition of this book it was reported that there were fewer females than males in professional sport. Whilst this is still true, and things continue to improve in this area, a disturbing trend has been highlighted by the Women's Sport and Fitness Foundation.[6] According to their research, a decreasing number of females are participating in active sport. In a 2010 report they noted a significant decrease, between 2007–08 and 2008–09, in female participation in regular sport (down 61,000 to 2.727 million) while men have seen an increase (up 176,600 to 4.203 million). Considering that 51% of the UK population is women, this is a disturbing statistic.

On the positive side, there have been encouraging increases in women taking part in athletics, netball and canoeing on a weekly basis, but conversely, there have been significant decreases in numbers of female swimmers, dance exercisers, gymnasts, skiers, squash players and those playing Rugby Union.

Although this doesn't necessarily mean that there will be fewer women earning a living out of competitive sport, it could mean that a smaller pool to draw from results in a drop in interest. Consequently this inevitable fall in viewing or reading figures could result in less input from sponsors.

In recognition of this downward trend the UK government has launched a Commission on the Future of Women's Sport specifically looking at:

- the lack of female leaders at the top level of sport;
- the poor promotion of women's sport both by the media and sport itself;
- the inequality of investment – both private and public funds.

The last of these topics may be difficult to prove unless things have changed significantly since the WSF (previous name of WSFF) last issued a report, (2006). Then they showed that 589 females received elite lottery funding, which was 48% of the overall total, even though women made up only around 17% of the membership of sporting organisations. The more recent research, above, by the WSF, also showed that these membership figures are on the decline. However, the figures do also seem to suggest that if so many female competitors receive Lottery funding (with its stringent eligibility rules) from such a small pool of competitors, then the quality of performance, by world standards, must be extremely high. Ergo, in this case, quantity doesn't mean quality.

Some women's sports, like football and rugby, despite greatly improving their profiles, lag way behind the men with regards to earnings. The England Women's Rugby team recently made the World Cup final where they were unfortunately beaten by the current world champions, New Zealand. The standard of performance from both teams was staggeringly high and yet there are no female professional players in England. All of the ladies representing the national team were either full-time students or holding down a full-time job, and fitting a very demanding training schedule around this. Remarkable.

As for soccer, despite making the most recent World Cup quarter finals, most of the women in the team fail to earn a living out of the sport. On arriving back from these championships in China, many of the team protested at the appallingly paltry £40 per day that they received. Players claimed fitness levels were suffering as they worked extra hours to claw back wages lost from their jobs.[7] However, they do get paid £400 a session for national squad training and other matches, with an extra £100 for personal appearances.

So things are steadily improving, but like most things, competitors are impatient, and want the situation to improve immediately. Alex Stone, who is the women's football representative on the FA, told BBC Radio 5 Live: 'The money that goes into women's football each year from the FA is currently at an all-time high – it's £4.5m.'

Working for a living

On a more positive note, however, in the sport and recreation sector in general, just over half of the workforce of 621,000 are female.[8] Typical salaries, after training, range from £20,000 to £35,000 p.a, and are obviously dependent on the type of job undertaken.

The scope for employment available in this sector ranges includes:

- club and duty management;
- sales and marketing;
- instructing and coaching;
- consultancy work based on GP referrals – e.g. diabetics, arthritics, etc.;
- osteopathy, naturopathy and chiropractic;
- lifestyle consultancy and nutrition;
- sport development and performance;
- administration and facility management;
- outdoor education;
- outdoor pursuits;
- sport media, including writing, PR and marketing;
- online games software development and business development;
- employment in holiday and caravan parks;
- roles within adventure tourism and gap year providers.

So the larger number of female employees here in some way counterbalances the disparity in professionals competing at sport, albeit that the wages in the sport and recreation sector are obviously lower in the short term, but are longer enduring and often also providing a pension.

Other advantages and disadvantages of working in this sector are the same for both men and women, and can be seen in Chapter 1; especially important are the charts (Figures 1 and 2).

Prize money

As stated previously, viewing figures and public interest have always dictated the amount of money that sponsors are willing to invest in a sport or specific event. A good example of this is shown by Rugby. In 2007 the total income for the Women's RFU was just under £2 million, whereas the men had £83 million pounds available to spend a year earlier.

With less interest in the Women's British Golf Open 2010 their winning prize money was £260,000 as opposed to £850,000 for the equivalent men's tournament.

The men do, however, play 72 holes as opposed to 56 for the ladies, but the disparity in prize money is still out of proportion. Although this gap could do with closing further, I'm sure that Yani Tseng, the female champion, will still be happy to deposit more than a quarter of a million pounds into her bank account.

This inequality in prize money is generally prevalent in most sports at their major championships. The one, however, that bucks the trend is tennis. The women's game at Wimbledon attracts almost the same viewing figures as the men's, and the organisers have recognised this by showing equality with their prize money.

The previous competition showed that the ladies only marginally lagged behind the men (£655k to £625k), but at this season's spectacular they achieved equality, with £850,000 each.

The men's British Open Golf Championship in 2010 was won by Louis Oosthuizen, who took home over $1 million (£850,000). Second place was Lee Westwood on £400,000. The prize money went all the way down to 77th place which was still worth a very acceptable £8200. Not a bad week's wage.

Don't forget, though, these were the best 77 golfers out of thousands who play the game around the world.

Unfortunately, the prize money for the ladies' game reflected the lesser media interest in this tournament, and also the fact that unlike Wimbledon, the men's and women's competitions are held at different venues, on different days. The winner, Yani Tseng, received approximately a quarter of the men's money on £260,000 and the prizes stretched down to 75th place on $1,563 (approximately £1,000).

LIVING ON PRIZE MONEY

Relying on prize money is a very risky way of making a living. The number of tournaments giving huge amounts of prize money are minimal, and the bigger the pot the more sportsmen, from all around the world, who will be chasing it. So your chances of success are minimal. Add to this the chance that at the time of this major tournament you may be injured, ill or off form, and you can see how risky it can be to rely on this way of financially supporting yourself, let alone a family. That said, tournaments often provide prize money for lower placed finishers as well as the winners, enabling 'professionals' to eke out a living merely by being 'placed' in competitions throughout the season.

What's available

Two good examples of the range of prize money available at major tournaments could be illustrated by the All England Tennis Championships, which is better known internationally simply as 'Wimbledon', and The British Open golf championships.

The total prize money given out at Wimbledon 2010 was £13,725,000, which was split equally between the men's and ladies' events.

The winners of the singles competitions received £1 million each, with the runners-up gaining £500K. Semi-finalists received £250,000 and quarter-finalists £125,000. Fourth-round qualifiers took home £62,500, whilst third-round £31,250, second-round £18,750 and first-round qualifiers received £11,250.

In the doubles events the winners received £240,000, with take-home earnings for first-round qualifiers of £5,250.

Even first-round losers in what is traditionally the lowest rewarded event, the mixed doubles, took home £2,600 (£1,300 each).

TAKING THE PLUNGE

If, despite the drawbacks stated above, you are still determined to make a career out of playing your sport, it would be prudent to:

* know your market;
* know your own ability;
* not aim too high;
* thoroughly research the opportunities.

Knowing your own ability

Competitors generally assess their ability in the context of the team they are currently playing with or, in the case of individual sports, the standard of tournament – local, county, national – that they are able to enter. Obviously, if you are only playing Sunday League football, or club tournament golf, there is little chance that any Football League clubs would be interested in you, or that you would make it through the qualifying tournaments for the British Open. However, strange things can happen, even the best selectors can get it wrong and your situation could be one of them.

When I was the County Schools Coach for under-19 basketball, I advised one of my better players to concentrate on his basketball, at which he had undoubted prospects. Unfortunately he preferred football and he was spending a lot of valuable training and basketball playing time pursuing his football dreams, even though he was only in his sixth form college's second team. He totally ignored my advice and went on to play for Middlesbrough FC and Manchester United. That student, Gary Pallister, also went on to play for England, and now since retirement still earns big money as a television pundit.

Being realistic

Occasionally, because of other influences, some prospective professional players can't gauge their ability through conventional methods because they have been out of the sport for a period of time. This could be due to injury, marriage, starting a family, work restrictions, or a multitude of other reasons. The first step in rehabilitation from any of these is primarily to get match fit, and then to approach a local club in order to test out their skills against various standards of competitor.

The golden rule is not to aim too high initially. Start at the bottom and work your way up. During this progression you will be gaining in fitness and improving your playing ability but also, just as importantly, you'll be acquiring knowledge initially of the local scene, then as you improve, the county and hopefully, later the national one.

Researching

Before embarking on any venture it is always wise to find out as much as possible about the market that interests you. Acquire a copy of your sport's specialist magazine, most large libraries carry the most popular of these, and also research it on the internet. Contact the magazines that interest you, and ask if they have printed any articles covering professionalism and opportunities in your sport. They will generally have back copies in stock, so will be pleased to furnish you with this information in order to make a sale.

The next step would then be to contact any clubs or associations mentioned in these articles that you think will be of assistance. Other useful sources of information can be local and national newspapers and local sports centres. Chapter 5 deals with this in greater detail.

If you are already playing at a high level you will probably already know someone who makes a living out of their sport and who knows what the terms of employment and 'work' conditions are like. If you don't know someone, ask around. Somebody in your club will no doubt have a contact who could help you.

Making your own opportunities

If, surprisingly, through your enquiries you don't uncover any opportunities, then try to make some for yourself. Place an advert on your club's noticeboard, in the local newsagents or at your sports centre. If these cheaper alternatives don't bear fruit you might consider splashing out on advertising in your sport's national magazine or on the internet. Let players and officials of your club, or rival clubs, know that you are looking for employment. You never know what may turn up. Once you have exhausted these avenues try writing to the national governing body of your sport. You can find the addresses of these organisations in Chapter 6.

CASE STUDY

The best time of Ian's life

Ian found playing much more attractive than coaching football.

He was one of the lucky few who went straight into a career as a pro footballer immediately after leaving school. His playing career began with Hartlepool United before transferring to Fulham. Later he joined Oxford United, but unfortunately an injury to his knee cut short his career, which nevertheless extended to more than ten years. Quite a good duration for a contact sport.

Nowadays Ian works at one of the local colleges as a football coach. He enjoys his job there, but obviously finds it very different from his playing career, which he describes as 'the best time of his life.'

Life in soccer was not only more glamorous and fun, but also the salary was a lot higher than he currently receives. Adapting to all of these changes was a real culture shock for him.

If he could make any changes, Ian would have completed all of his coaching awards whilst still playing. This would have enabled him to take up the many offers he received to stay in professional sport.

Ian also advises any youngsters thinking of pursing this option to go for it 100 per cent, *but* not to forget that at some time it is going to end, so look after the money!

Ian gained the first FA coaching badge before retiring from soccer and is now nearing completing his final one. After this he is considering possibly changing tack and qualifying as a teacher.

TAKING THE PLUNGE – CHECKLIST

◆ Know your market – do you thoroughly understand the complexities of the sport that you are hoping to work in?

◆ Know your ability – are you good enough to make the grade? Dreams alone won't do it.

◆ Don't aim too high, too soon – take your time and use that time constructively.

◆ Research – magazines, guides, brochures, newspapers, internet, etc.

◆ Enquire – through teammates, opponents, coaches, administrators, etc.

◆ Advertise – on noticeboards, sports magazines, newspapers, the internet, etc.

◆ Contact – local and national organisers.

COACHING AND INSTRUCTING

You can gain valuable experience coaching and instructing sportspeople without holding a recognised qualification, but this is not recommended. First of all it will be almost impossible to gain paid employment without one, but more importantly you will not be covered if somebody injures themselves (participants and spectators) in one of your sessions. If you hold a recognised coaching award it is almost 100 per cent certain that they will provide you with insurance cover for free, or in some cases at very low cost.

To achieve the basic level coaching award is very easy in most sports, and this is dealt with in more detail in Chapter 7. A list of organisers of these awards is contained in Chapter 6.

Where is the demand?

The demand for coaches varies both in the UK and abroad, but as a general rule there are always opportunities for employment in:

◆ sports centres and swimming baths;
◆ private sports clubs (soccer, tennis, squash, fitness, etc.);
◆ outdoor pursuits centres;
◆ local authorities (sports development officer, management, etc.);
◆ commercial organisations (ski companies, activity holiday companies, etc.).

CASE STUDY

Gareth loves his job as a golf pro

Gareth's mother and father were both keen golfers and took him for his first game when he was about seven years old. From then on he was hooked.

Gareth was good at a multitude of other sports including cricket, skiing and soccer and even started a sports science degree at university, but it was golf that was his first love. He was playing county golf and had won numerous tournaments when he decided to try his luck on the Euro Pro Tour. Unfortunately this didn't work out as he was earning barely enough money to live on, so he pursued the next option working as a club pro.

He took the PGA National Diploma, which involves everything from teaching to sports science and club repair, and is an absolute requirement for this work.

After qualifying Gareth became one of the Club Professionals at Wynyard Golf Club where he loves his job. He easily makes enough money to live on, but this fluctuates with the season. He is paid only a small basic wage for running the pro shop, but gets a commission on sales. He is also really pleased that at this club he keeps all fees for teaching, whereas at other clubs the head pro normally takes a big percentage of these.

So Gareth is really happy with his career, as not only does it provide him with a good living wage, but also gives him the opportunity to play as much golf as he wants. He also loves many other aspects of the game: the fact that you never stop learning, the social side of it, travelling around Britain and Europe to other courses, seeing people who he has coached, especially kids, develop and meeting so many interesting people.

Gareth would advise anybody considering golf as a career to first of all be realistic, and consider if they are good enough. He has seen so many fail because they thought they were better than they actually were.

Then they should decide early which direction they are going to take. Try for a golf scholarship, if they have the ability. If they are going to try out as a tournament pro they should go at it 100 per cent as they can always take their PGA awards at a later date, and the experience that they have gained will always be useful.

WORKING IN SPORTS-RELATED EMPLOYMENT

There are numerous jobs connected with sport which, although you might not be taking part directly in your own sport, may prove satisfying merely by being associated with it. For example:

- community recreation officer;
- county development officer;
- groundsman;
- manager of a leisure facility;
- sports manufacturer's rep;
- outdoor activities instructor;
- P.E. teacher;
- physiotherapist;
- retail manager/assistant;
- sports centre assistant;
- sports journalist;
- sports photographer.

CASE STUDY
Working at a leisure facility

Jim had worked at numerous jobs including in the NHS, the NAAFI and Qantas, before gaining employment in the leisure sector. Conversely, Ian had taken employment in leisure straight after leaving school, initially working in swimming pools and sports centres. They now both form part of the management team at a large leisure facility/athletics stadium.

Jim's official title is Principal Leisure Manager, and Ian is Recreation Officer. They both agree that they prefer their present jobs to anything they have done previously, but for different reasons.

Ian originally intended joining the army, but is glad he didn't as he now gets a lot of pleasure working with the public.

Jim prefers this job because of the variety. The hours are long, but the rewards are there. He wanted to point out that the job also has its downsides, like dealing with irate customers and slow bureaucracy. Nevertheless, he still enjoys it.

Ian advises anybody considering this as a career to look in the weekly ILAM bulletins (see Glossary) or local newspapers for situations vacant. You don't need any qualifications to begin with, but a certificate in first aid would give you a head start. Once employed you would be trained on the job, and expected to take courses such as safe electricity at work, and handling aggression and violence.

TEACHING

Many schoolchildren are inspired towards a career in sport by their own P.E. teacher. They probably get the impression that the P.E. teacher's job entails running around playing sport all day with the pupils. In fact nothing could be further from the truth. The P.E. teacher's workload generally consists of the following.

+ Being a form teacher; registering their class and taking them to assembly every morning.

+ Dealing with any classwork, homework, discipline and truancy problems.

+ Taking lessons in sport, but probably also the second teaching subject that they trained in.

- Collecting in valuables, dealing with lost kit and suspiciously examining sick notes.

- Filling in assessment forms for every pupil in every class.

- Writing reports for all of their pupils.

- Giving up lunchtimes, evenings and weekends, without extra pay, to run school teams.

- Attending staff meetings, as well as those for faculties, departments and houses.

- Attending parents' evenings.

- Lesson preparation and marking coursework.

- Telephoning parents and other schools for fixtures.

- Administering first aid.

- Ordering new equipment and maintaining the old.

You can see that a lot of the P.E. teacher's workload is taken up by doing work that is not directly connected to sport. The most enjoyable part is taking the children for lessons, but this only accounts for a fraction of the time, and remember this is *teaching*, not actually participating in sport. In fact a directive sent out by the Department of Education several years ago stated quite categorically that teachers should not join in any contact sports with the children. Contact sports included soccer, basketball and hockey amongst others.

So the opportunities for P.E. teachers to play sports and maintain their level of skill and fitness, within lesson times, is very limited.

Nevertheless, P.E. teaching is a very satisfying and rewarding job.

Qualifications

In order to teach you need to have acquired the appropriate teaching qualification at university. This is normally a Bachelor of Education degree, or a PGCE for graduates already possessing a degree. Before being accepted at university, applicants will need to have passed at least two A levels. P.E. teachers will also be expected to have achieved a high level of proficiency in at least one sport.

CASE STUDY

Kath made a career-changing choice

Kath played hockey for the South of Scotland, and had experienced all sorts of part-time jobs before settling on a career. Amongst these she worked in a petrol station, fast-food outlet and the Edinburgh Festival; and she was very glad that she did.

Her original intention had been to go to university to study law, but after these jobs she realised that she was more of a 'people person' and decided to ignore the lucrative wages of the legal profession, and become a teacher.

She qualified with a Bachelor of Education degree from Heriot-Watt University and then travelled south to take her first teaching job amongst the sassenachs – she even married one, a fellow teacher at her first school in Cleveland.

Kath has now moved on to teach at a private school in the same town, but says that she has never regretted the decisions she took about her career. She loves working with children, running around in the fresh air, and the fact that in this job, every day is slightly different.

She wouldn't change much about her life, but if she had the time over again would have included a sports physiotherapy qualification in with her course. She would probably also have taken her coaching qualifications to the highest level possible.

Her advice to anyone considering going into P.E. teaching is to first concentrate on their own sport, and take this to the highest level that they possibly can. Then, to look around a good sports-orientated university, like Loughborough, to see what is involved in all aspects of this profession. It may be that research or coaching, or physiotherapy is a more suitable move for them.

THE ARMED FORCES

One of the Army's past adverts read:

> Who encourages you to play sport during working hours? *The Army does.*

This confirms one of the great attractions of a services career to sportspeople. The higher level that you play your sport at, the more time you'll get off to pursue it. In other words you are being paid to play sport.

Unfortunately, it's not quite as simple as that and there are other demands and responsibilities that come with a services career. Amongst others you could be asked to serve in a war zone.

Also:

◆ You have to be able to cope with living in a barracks with other recruits.

◆ You have to be able to cope with discipline.

◆ You normally have to complete basic training before you qualify for time off to play any sport.

If you join the Navy remember that competing in your sport is very difficult if you are on board a ship. The Army and the RAF are therefore able to provide greater opportunities for sporting achievement as they offer more land based careers.

Becoming a Physical Training Instructor (PTI) isn't absolutely necessary to pursue your sport. Sometimes it is better to work in another trade, leaving yourself fresh and enthusiastic for participation. It also gives you another avenue of opportunity to pursue when your sports career is over.

CASE STUDY
Playing to the max in the Army
I met Doug at a county rugby match and was immediately interested in his role in the Armed Forces in relation to his participation in sport. His job in the Army was as a mechanic with the Royal Engineers, but he was given time off to partake in his representative sports. He not only played county rugby, but also for his regiment, the Army and the Combined Services. For each of these he was given leave to train and play. He was currently only working for two and a half days per week, but told me that he had just made the regiment's basketball team and so expected to spend even less time on base.

I was seriously considering joining up myself but a tour of duty in Afghanistan put me off!

TAKING A YEAR (OR MORE) OUT
The vast majority of students who decide to take a year out generally want to see the world and earn money at the same time. Chapter 4 looks at the different options abroad. However, some students prefer to stay in Britain for this study break. The

reasons for doing so vary, but some of the main ones are as follows:

1. They want to gain experience in industry before embarking on university or college.

2. They simply want a short break from the educational system before returning to working and studying for exams.

3. They want to pursue their sport to a higher level without the burden of exams or a career.

4. They want to earn some money before becoming a penniless student at university.

CASE STUDY

Steve decides that studying could get in the way

After leaving school Steve had arranged a year's work experience in industry through the Year in Industry scheme run by Durham University. After this he intended to study at Sheffield University for a degree in electrical engineering and electronics. He had decided on this course of action because:

◆ He wanted a break from the pressures of theory work and exams.

◆ It would help him in future job applications to have this experience behind him.

◆ He wanted to earn some money before becoming an impoverished student.

◆ He wanted to train for athletics.

Steve had one last chance to become an international athlete at Junior Men's level. It would be much harder the following year when he moves up into the Senior ranks. He had been highly placed in the National Decathlon rankings the previous year when he was a year younger than most of the athletes above him. This season was his last chance; now it was all or nothing.

When interviewed Steve reflected on his decision. He thought that he had made the right decision to take a year out to train for athletics but, if he had the time over again, he would not have taken the same job. He would have worked part-time as putting so much effort into his work often left him too tired to train properly. Otherwise he had no regrets.

Unfortunately, Steve didn't gain his international vest as a serious injury whilst pole vaulting cut short his season. After qualifying Steve also decided that engineering was not for him, and now earns a fortune as a mortgage advisor.

STUDYING WHILST COACHING AND COMPETING

Gaining a place at college or university is an ideal way of participating in and improving your sport. The added bonus is that you come out at the end of your course with a qualification that many employers find desirable.

Sports scholarships started, and are still nowadays predominantly available, in the USA. However other countries, including Britain, are quickly catching up with their system.

Since the last edition of this book there have been significant changes in the funding of our better sportspeople who choose to pursue a course of higher education whilst competing. It is still, however, nowhere near as financially rewarding as it is in the USA and there is still no structured national directive on this. It is also left to individual universities and colleges to decide whether or not they want to offer scholarships and/or bursaries to talented sportspeople.

Most British universities now also offer the Talented Athlete Scholarship, which is enlarged upon below.

The TASS scheme

The Talented Athlete Scholarship Scheme (TASS) was made possible, on the whole, by a major advancement in funding organised by the government and sports councils. The word 'Athlete' in the title is used in its broadest sense, unfortunately imported from America, to mean sportsmen and sportswomen, as opposed to the English 'Athlete', which in the USA is referred to as track and field athletes. The TASS scheme supports about 50 sports in total, ranging from Archery to Waterskiing, and approximately 30% of these are disability sports. To quote their website:

TASS is a unique partnership between National Governing Bodies of sport and Educational Institutions, designed especially to cater for the needs of athletes within the education system during higher and further education.

The TASS programme has been created to help hundreds to fulfill their sporting potential by maintaining a sensible balance between academic life or employment whilst training and competing as a performance athlete. TASS aims to reduce the drop-out of talented athletes from sport due to academic and financial pressures.

TASS athletes that are awarded a scholarship will receive sporting support and services to the value of £3,500, and those awarded a TASS 2012 Scholarship will receive sporting support and services up to the value of £10,000.

TASS awards are made annually, to cover the academic year, October to the following September.

To be eligible for an award candidates must:

◆ have a British Passport;

◆ be undertaking a course at a recognised educational institution in England, unless you are a TASS 2012 athlete and then your course can be in a recognised educational institution anywhere;

◆ be up to the standard to represent either Great Britain or England in thcir choscn sport.

You must also be nominated by your educational institute and approved by your NGB (national governing body).

Athletes already in receipt of world-class funding (e.g. Talent, Development and Podium) are not eligible.

If you want more information on this scheme click onto the TASS website at: www.tass.gov.uk

As well as offering TASS, many colleges and universities offer their own scholarships or bursaries. Detailed below is a list of what was recently on offer in the UK. It is by no means a definitive list and many details may have changed since going to press. So if you are interested in a particular university or college, check out their own prospectus or website.

In most cases it will be sufficient to type 'Sports Scholarships' into their 'search' facility.

Scholarships and bursaries that have recently been available

- Aberdeen University
  Up to 20 sports bursaries are awarded each year plus two scholarships worth £1,250 and £3,000 respectively. For more information: www.abdn.ac.uk

- Aberystwyth University
  Offers sports bursaries of £500 p.a., plus guaranteed accommodation in halls of residence, plus free access to the university sports centre, to students who have achieved a high standard in their sport. For more information: www.aber.ac.uk

- Bangor University
  Has a number of sport scholarships available, worth up to £2,000 a year each. The scholarships are not be restricted to any particular sport. For more information: www.bangor.ac.uk

- University of Bath
  Offers numerous awards through TASS worth £3,000 p.a. and also has several sport scholarships available, worth up to £2,000 a year through Team Bath. For more information: www.bath.ac.uk

- University of Birmingham
  Over 40 sports scholarship and bursaries are awarded each year. For more information go to www.sport.bham.ac.uk

- University of Bristol
  Twelve awards of £3,000 are made each year, plus a rowing scholarship and The Lloyd Robinson Sports Scholarship, both of up to £1,000, plus TASS. For more information: www.bris.ac.uk

- Brunel University
  Numerous scholarships and bursaries are awarded each year in
  20 SportEngland priority sports each year. The university
  doesn't quantify exact figures. For more information:
  www.brunel.ac.uk

- University of Cambridge
  A multitude of scholarships and bursaries are on offer through
  individual colleges. The link given below is for Selwyn College
  which, even if unsuitable, should point towards information on
  other colleges. For more information: www.sel.cam.ac.uk/
  alumni/GivingtoSelwyn/sportsbursaryscheme.html

- Cardiff University
  Although a range of advantages to receiving one of their
  bursaries is quoted, the university's website only states
  'possible financial reward'. For more information contact them
  personally at: www.cardiff.ac.uk

- Coventry University
  Up to 50 sports scholarships are awarded per year, each worth
  up to £1,500 in cash and an extra £1500 in services.
  For more information: www.coventry.ac.uk

- De Montfort University
  An unlimited number of alumni scholarships of £500 are on
  offer. For more information: www.dmu.ac.uk

- Durham University
  A minimum of 25 vice-chancellor's sports scholarships per
  year worth £2,000 are offered. For more information:
  www.dur.ac.uk

- Edinburgh University
  More than 170 new bursaries each year worth a minimum of

£1,000, plus at least 32 scholarships for varying amounts (not solely for sport) are on offer. Sports bursaries vary from £350 to specialist golf ones of £1,500. For more information: www.ed.ac.uk

◆ University of Exeter
More than 40 scholarships, on average, are awarded each year. These include cash from £500 up to £2,000 for exceptional athletes plus the equivalent of £500 in support packages. Also on offer are bursaries in golf and rugby. For more information: sport.exeter.ac.uk

◆ Glasgow University
In addition to the athlete support services available to talented athletes, the Colin Montgomerie Golf Scholarship of £400 and other golf scholarships of unspecified quantity are available. For more information:www.gla.ac.uk

◆ Heriot-Watt University
Offers support in the region of £2,000 to athletes considered to be of national standard in any of their 32 sports union sports. For more information: www.hw.ac.uk

◆ Leeds Metropolitan University
Offers Carnegie Scholarships (as well as TASS) to high level athletes but are not specific about the amount of cash involved. For more information contact through their website: www.leedsmet.ac.uk

◆ Loughborough University
Offers £1,000 cash towards living expenses as well as up to £3,000 towards tuition fees and £250 towards campus facility hire/memberships. For more information: www.lboro.ac.uk

- University of Manchester
  Offers up to £500 cash and support services that total a maximum of £2,000. For more information: www.sport.manchester.ac.uk

- Newcastle University
  Awards up to 40 sports scholarships each year. Performance Scholarships are worth £1,000, and Recruitment Scholarships are awarded at three levels but the cash amounts are not given. More information: www.ncl.ac.uk

- University of Northumbria
  Awards, as well as TASS, only general scholarships to students which are worth £250. For more information: www.northumbria.ac.uk

- University of Oxford
  Surprisingly there are only four scholarships available to university sports players. The best of these is only £600 with possible further discretionary awards of bursaries for kit and travel. In addition there are eight Oxford University society awards which offer support for sporting projects; these are worth £250 each. For further information: www.sport.ox.ac.uk/sports-federation/scholarships

- Queen's University Belfast
  Offer a number of bursaries to high-achieving athletes. However, they don't specify the quantity.
  For more information you are advised to email: k.oakes@qub.ac.uk

- University of Reading
  Twenty-two different scholarships, bursaries and prizes are listed on their website, which are awarded, on an annual basis, for all subjects. The sports-specific scholarships are for all

sports with the main focus being rowing, rugby and golf, and range from £500 to £2,000. More information: www.reading.ac.uk

◆ St Andrew's University
Makes awards on two levels: one for Sports Scholars, for golf, and secondly for Talented Athletes. Amounts and quantities are not disclosed. For further information contact: www.st-andrews.ac.uk

◆ Stirling University
Awards scholarships in five core sports: golf, football, swimming, tennis and triathlon. The Craig Gowans football scholarship is worth £2,500. For details of this and other awards, contact: www.external.stir.ac.uk

◆ University of Strathclyde
Awards bursaries of up to £1,000, in two areas: the University Golf Programme and the University Sports Bursary Programme for a wide range of sports. For more information: www.strath.ac.uk

◆ University of Sunderland
Awards general scholarships of up to £1,050 p.a. but don't state that any are sport-specific. For more information: www.sunderland.ac.uk

◆ University of Surrey
Operates the government's Talented Athlete Scholarship Scheme (mentioned earlier in the book) but doesn't provide sports scholarships over and above this. For more information: portal.surrey.ac.uk

◆ Swansea University
Offers ten sports scholarships each year which are worth

£1,000. Full details are available from
g.m.jones@swansea.ac.uk

◆ Teesside University
Awards 40 scholarships for excellence which, to quote them,
'could be worth more than £14,000 over three years' but these
are all academically based. Students wanting to link study with
their sport are still eligible to apply if they have the high
academic achievements required. For more information:
www.tees.ac.uk

◆ University of Ulster
Although Ulster doesn't state on its website the size of their
scholarships, they offer an impressive 53 of them, including 23
dedicated to Outreach Sport, 10 dedicated to promoting
Women in Sport and two specifically for promoting disability
sport. For more information: www.ulster.ac.uk

◆ University of Wales
Has numerous scholarships on offer but none appear to be
sport-specific. For more information: www.wales.ac.uk

◆ University of Wales, Newport
Has sports scholarships and bursaries on offer, but do not
stipulate what their provision is on their website.
For further information: www.newport.ac.uk

◆ University of Worcester
Offers University Scholarships of up to £2,000 p.a. for elite
sport. More information on: www.worcester.ac.uk

COACHING AND RESEARCH OPPORTUNITIES WITHIN COLLEGES

The American system of offering 'Graduate Assistantships' (GAs)
to postgraduates wanting to continue pursuing their sport whilst

either furthering their own education, or teaching/coaching other students has been adopted in Britain, but to a lesser extent. In the USA almost every college/university, with very few exceptions, offers GAs to their most talented athletes, but it is more of a rarity in the UK.

Within the last few years, several British universities have advertised openings for graduate sportsmen/women. Although these positions have since been filled they can still be a useful illustration of the types of opportunities that could be available.

Loughborough University required for October 2010 at the School of Sport Exercise and Health Sciences a research associate in exercise physiology/biochemistry. The stipend ranged between £27,319 to £35,646 per annum for a fixed term of three years.

The University of Bath funds seven post-doctoral research officers and 17 postgraduate research students. Their most recently available post was for several graduate teaching assistants. They were required for January 2010 and had to be PhD students who could assist with teaching. The funding consisted of a studentship maintenance stipend (currently £9,950 per annum) and a salary (currently £5,850 per annum) with annual increments.

Although Brunel University doesn't currently have a PhD studentship (as they call it) available in sport-related research, they do offer annually a generous research scholarship scheme for up to 15 PhD students *across the full range of subjects*. These are funded for three years to cover all fees plus at least £13,290 per year maintenance grant and £1000 per year research training grant.

Graduate assistantships have also been available in recent years at the Universities of Manchester and Leeds Metropolitan.

If you would like more information on these types of positions, you will find the individual university's website address earlier in this chapter. Otherwise for general, or more up to date, information contact: British Universities & Colleges Sport (BUCS) *(formerly BUSA)*, 20–24 Kings Bench Street, London SE1 0QX Tel: 020 7633 5080 website: www.bucs.org.uk/

WORKING IN CLOSE PROXIMITY TO YOUR SPORT

Working in a job that keeps you close to your sport, without actually participating, can be a good idea as it maintains your interest and freshness. There are countless opportunities, too numerous to mention, in every type of employment. So if you are interested in this option you need to first choose the region where you would like to be involved in sport, then the area in which you can obtain accommodation and then try to gain employment somewhere between the two.

Your first task must be to contact the Jobcentre in that area to find out the range of jobs that are available. If nothing appeals to you then you could try contacting the sports club that you are intending joining, and even opposing clubs who might be interested in 'stealing' your services by offering a lucrative job. If they suggest that you visit them you could use this as an opportunity to check out:

- noticeboards at the local sports centres;
- noticeboards at youth hostels;
- situations vacant in the local newspapers;
- specialist newspapers and magazines connected to your sport.

You could also take the opportunity to place your own advert when visiting these places, plus other places such as supermarkets and shops, offering your services.

VOLUNTARY WORK

Although many people considering voluntary work are interested in working abroad, it is also possible to pursue this course in Britain. Hospitals and care centres rely on this type of help, and organisations such as Help the Aged and Oxfam often have vacancies for volunteers, many of these offering expenses.

You will find this option is covered more extensively in Chapter 4. Although it deals with working abroad, much of the advice is also relevant to Britain. The suggested reading is particularly important if you are considering this as a way forward.

SELF-ASSESSMENT EXERCISE

1. Have you decided that it is definitely Britain that you want to work in?

2. Which option of utilising your sport most appeals to you?

3. Do you have the required level of skill and qualifications to enable you to follow this path?

4. Do you know who to contact to pursue your chosen sport?

3

Working at the Olympics

The XXX Summer Olympiad will be held in London from 27 July to 12 August 2012, followed by the Paralympic Games from the 29 August to 9 September. The organisation for these events was put into the hands of LOCOG (The London Organising Committee of the Olympic Games) shortly after their bid was successful and in July 2005.

Hosting an Olympic Games is an enormous undertaking. It also provides a huge opportunity for employment.

The vast majority of specialist workers, competitors, coaches, managers, etc., were identified at least four years ago and have been working throughout this time towards success at these games.

Although it *has* been known for an Olympic star to suddenly appear from nowhere and then, at the last possible minute, gain selection for the games, this is as rare as winning the National Lottery. However, if you have a talent for a sport and you think you fall into this category then you must start working hard at it immediately. Most sports have yet to hold their Olympic trials. These are normally held at the end of 2011 or start of the following year, to finalise their selection for London 2012. The first thing you must do in this case is to get involved with a good coach and/or a good club. Details of how to do so are in Chapter 6.

Soon after LOCOG was established, the locations and sites were identified, and the first contractors were selected to build new venues and the other necessary infrastructure. Obviously all of this created new jobs for the wider public.

Below is an illustration of the huge diversity of jobs that have been created. Details of only a small number of them that were available in late 2010 are given. It is unlikely that these vacancies are still unfilled – however, it is still worth checking. Even if these jobs have gone, it is likely that the agency whose web address is given will have similar ones.

JOBS AVAILABLE PRIOR TO THE LONDON OLYMPICS

Construction industry

Senior Quantity Surveyor	Olympics	construction-jobs.ie
Civils Site Agent for the Olympics	London	reed.co.uk
Metal Studworker for the Olympics	Stratford, Essex	gumtree.co.uk
OlympicVillage Construction Workers	Stratford, Essex	gumtree.co.uk
Dumper Drivers	Olympic Park	reed.co.uk
Site Fitter	Olympic Site	cv-library.co.uk
Mechanical Supervisor	Athletes Village	engineerboard.co.uk

Management

Head of Summer Sport Engagement	BOA, London	uksport.gov.uk
Sport Engagement Manager	BOA, London	uksport.gov.uk
Boxing Services Manager	Canary Wharf, London	uksport.gov.uk
Fencing Services Manager	Canary Wharf, London	uksport.gov.uk
Rowing Services Manager	Canary Wharf, London	uksport.gov.uk
Synchronised Swimming Manager	Canary Wharf, London	uksport.gov.uk
Table Tennis Services Manager	Canary Wharf, London	uksport.gov.uk
Taekwondo Tech. Operations Manager	Canary Wharf, London	uksport.gov.uk
Triathlon Services Manager	Canary Wharf, London	uksport.gov.uk
Weightlifting Tech. Operations Manager	Canary Wharf, London	uksport.gov.uk
Olympic Venue General Managers	Various across UK	uksport.gov.uk

Technical Manager – Telecoms	Canary Wharf	london2012.com
Games Operations Co-ordinator	B. Paralympic Assn. London	uksport.gov.uk
Event Project Manager	London Area	onlymarketingjobs.com
Villages Housekeeping Manager	Various	london2012.com
Sponsorship Director for Olympics	Global	onlymarketingjobs.com
Marketing Manager	Tower Hamlets	civilservice.gov.uk
Venue General Managers	Various	london2012.com
Venue Retail Precinct Manager	Canary Wharf	london2012.com

Miscellaneous

Creative Division Administrator	Olympic Stadium	london2012.com
Head of Security	Olympic Site	london2012.com
Regional Coordinator for Africa	Canary Wharf	london2012.com
Public Enquiries Executive	Canary Wharf	london2012.com
Junior Administrator	Olympic site	justlondonjobs.co.uk
Copywriter – Sports Operations	Canary Wharf	london2012.com
Publications Assistant	Canary Wharf	london2012.com
Minibus Driver	Olympic Site	jobsite.co.uk
College and Community Football Co-ordinator	Manchester	Blue Octopus Recruitment Ltd
Solicitor for Olympic Development	Olympic Park	www.veredus.co.uk

In early July 2010 LOCOG announced plans to recruit up to 70,000 volunteers for the Olympics and Paralympics, in the biggest post-war volunteer recruitment campaign in the UK's history.

The volunteers, known as Games Makers, will be vital in ensuring the smooth running of the Games. LOCOG will be looking for inspirational and dedicated people to fill one of the two different types of roles:

Specialists – in areas such as medical services, sport or press operations, etc.; and

Generalists – whose roles range from spectator assistants, uniform distributors, ticket checking, etc.

Volunteer recruitment started on 27 July 2010, for Specialists, and on 15 September for Generalists.

They are keen to recruit volunteers from all backgrounds and from areas of the UK. However, applicants must be over 18 on 1 January 2012 (unless applying as a Junior Games Maker – see below) and must be eligible to work in the UK.

They must also be available to work at least ten days during the Games and to do at least three days' training.

On the downside volunteers must find their own accommodation and transport. This might not be too cheap if you are interested in one of the sports held in London but live outside the capital.

From my own experience, I have found that local families are often willing to offer free (or very cheap) accommodation to the type of person that volunteers. I have in the past done so twice myself for similar sporting projects. This, however, cannot be relied on and you should have other arrangements in place – just in case.

Don't forget, though, that as well as London, Olympic and Paralympic events are held at nine other venues outside the capital. Details of these, and an outline of the events held there, are given later in this chapter, or more extensively on the LOCOG website.

LOCOG have also confirmed that up to 1,500 of the Games Maker roles will be made available for those under the age of 18 through the 'Young Games Maker' programme but details of these will not be unveiled until July 2011.

SELECTING THE RIGHT SORT OF PERSON TO BE A GAMES MAKER

LOCOG have compiled a list of the qualities that they consider that Games Makers will need to possess if they are to be successful in their job. You don't need to possess *every* quality, but possessing *most of them* will be desirable. They are:

- energetic;
- inspirational;
- reliable;
- good-natured;
- openness and honesty;
- respectful;
- patient;
- understanding;
- resilience;
- co-operative;
- supportive;
- the ability to deal with the unexpected – work as part of a team – and the willingness to go the extra mile.

Be aware though, that it is anticipated that only approximately 10% of applicants will be successful, so if you don't possess the majority of the above qualities, you will have little chance of success. The organisers of the Beijing Olympics 2008 received more than one million applications for their voluntary jobs!

Games Makers, by the very nature of their roles will be the 'faces' of the Games. The 'Specialists' will know their jobs and roles intimately, but 'Generalists' will be at the centre of everything else. The work will be very demanding. They will need to be energetic. They will inspire everyone they meet and fill them with the 'spirit' of the Olympic and Paralympic Games. They will need to be understanding, open and honest in everything they do.

They will need patience and be respectful in dealing with questions and requests from people from many other cultures from all four corners of the world. They must ensure that no one is excluded.

Literally thousands of Games Makers will have to work together to ensure the smooth running of these Games, so teamwork is absolutely vital.

All in all, not an easy job, so what can you expect to get from this work? Well, apart from extreme tiredness, satisfaction in doing a great, worthwhile job. You will likely build new friendships and develop new skills that will be appreciated by future employers, and look great on a CV.

An added bonus to this is that you will get an official uniform to wear during your shifts – which you get to keep as a memento after everything has finished.

It must also be noted though, that Games Makers are not entitled to free tickets or backstage passes.

An online application form can be found on the LOCOG website: www.london2012.com, where you can also find more expansive details.

You can, on the application form, indicate where and how you would like to volunteer, but the organisers cannot guarantee that all these requests will be able to be met. Details are given on the above website of all the different roles and areas that are available.

There will be 31 different 'Teams' or 'Functional Areas' in ten different locations available. As the website is interactive, and easy to use, I suggest that you access this, as it would be impossible in a (non-interactive) book to illustrate the full extent of the combinations of roles available, and in which areas they are sited.

It is possible, however, to list the ten different areas in which volunteers are required. They are (from north to south):

Glasgow	Hampden Park	Co-Host of the Football Competitions
Newcastle	St James's Park	Co-Host of the Football Competitions
Manchester	Old Trafford	Co-Host of the Football Competitions
Coventry	City of C. Stadium	Co-Host of the Football Competitions
Lee Valley	White Water Centre	Venue for the Canoe Slalom
London	Wembley Stadium	Co-Host of the Football Competitions
London	Wembley Arena	Badminton and Rhythmic Gymnastics
London	Regents Park	Finish of the Road Cycling Events
London	Eton Manor	Training for Aquatics/Wheelchair Tennis
London	Basketball Arena	All Basketball, Handball and Wheelchair Rugby
London	Velo Park	Track Cycling and BMX Events
London	Hockey Centre	Hockey + 5-a-side and 7-a-side Football
London	IBC and MPC	24 hour Press and Media hub
London	Olympic Village	Accommodation Shops, Restaurants, Medical, etc.
London	Handball Arena	Prelim. rounds of Handball Competition
London	Aquatics Centre	Swimming, Diving
London	Olympic Stadium	Opening/Closing Ceremonies and Athletics
London	Royal Artillery Barracks	Venue for some Shooting and Archery
London	Lord's Cricket Ground	Venue for some Archery
London	Horse Guards Parade	Temporary Venue for Beach Volleyball
London	UDAC	Uniform Distribution and Accreditation
London	N. Greenwich Arena	Gymnastics, Trampoline and Basketball Finals
London	Greenwich Park	Equestrian and Modern Pentathlon Events
London	ExCel	Boxing, Fencing, Judo, Table Tennis, Weights, etc.
London	Wimbledon	Venue for Tennis
Eton	E. Dorney Rowing Centre	Venue for Rowing and Canoe Sprints

Hadleigh	Hadleigh Farm	Venue for Mountain Bike Events
Cardiff	Millennium Stadium	Co-Host of the Football Competitions
Weymouth	and Portland Bay	Sailing Competitions

More precise information on the venues and the events held there can, of course, be found on the LOCOG website: www.london2012.com

Equally, on the same website, you can find information on the roles required at each venue and the times and dates they will be required.

Precise details of each volunteering job is also on the website, but their broad titles are listed below:

Accommodation, Accreditation, Anti-Doping, Brand Protection, Catering, Cleaning and Waste, Client Services, Community Relations, Editorial Services, Event Services, Government Relations, Information and Knowledge Management, Media and Public Relations, Medical, National Olympic Committee and National Paralympic Committee Services and Relations, Olympic and Paralympic Family Services, Opening and Closing Ceremonies, Press Operations, Protocol and Language Services, Sport, Rate Card, Sustainability, Technology, Ticketing, Torch, Transport, Venue Management, Victory Ceremonies, Village Management, Uniforms, Website and New Media, Workforce Operations.

So, as you can see, it is a phenomenal undertaking.

Different Games Makers are required at each venue in differing numbers and over different periods of time. The combination of these is far too complex to explain here, but is comprehensively dealt with, in an easy to understand manner, on the LOCOG website.

Most positions have already been taken – but some are still available. They are, understandably, going fast – so act quickly.

The online application form for any of the above positions should take only 30 to 40 minutes fill in. This section of the website also goes into greater detail about the timescale of events once your form has been received.

In addition to the above, the Mayor of London plans to spend £19.6 million on providing work for Londoners. This will mainly take the form of 'London Volunteers' but other paid employment will be available. Employment in the five Olympics host boroughs is well below the national average, but the London Olympics are expected to create 173,000 job opportunities. These will include volunteers and short-term jobs but it is hoped that a positive employment legacy will be left long after the Games have finished.

Most of the jobs created will be centred on key transport hubs, visitor attractions and on the streets of the capital during the Games to ensure that visitors receive the best possible welcome experience and impression of the City.

Recruitment for these posts also started on 27 July 2010 and more expansive details can be found on the Lord Mayor's website at www.london.gov.uk

If you are not sure if volunteering is for you, read the information on the above site and also read the section on 'Voluntary Work in Great Britain' in Chapter 2 of this book.

4
Examining the Different Options Abroad

Working abroad is sometimes the preferred option of many sportspeople as not only does it give them the opportunity to enjoy paid employment in their favourite sport, but also they gain experience in coaching or playing in a different environment. Further benefits are also gaining useful references, which can be utilised when seeking employment back at home, while at the same time experiencing different cultures.

PLAYING AWAY

Becoming wealthy through your sport abroad is not easy. David Beckham and Michael Owen are the exceptions rather than the rule. You need to be absolutely outstanding to be a top earner whatever your sport! You don't, however, need to be *that* good if your aim is just to use your sport as an opportunity to travel, or earn a moderate living whilst experiencing a different environment.

Choosing the right country

If your chosen sport is soccer and you want to play abroad then don't expect to be snapped up by teams in Europe or South America – they *will* expect you to be brilliant! But if you tried a club in Asia, Africa, or North America your chances would be much better.

Alternatively, if your sport is rugby, which few countries in the world play better than Britain, then approaching clubs in Europe or the Americas could be advantageous.

The best course of action is always to be realistic in your aims and to follow the procedure we introduced in Chapter 2:

- know your market;
- know your own ability;
- research;
- don't aim too high.

CASE STUDY
Stu swaps Stockton for Michigan

Stu had hit a crossroads in his life. His current job was only OK, but his rugby career was on the slide. He also felt that he had not done enough or seen enough of the world. He was quite a typical case.

He had left school to go straight to university and then, once qualified, back to school again; this time teaching.

So he decided to call in an offer that he had received whilst at college, and at the end of the summer holidays boarded a plane for Detroit.

Stu played rugby for Michigan RFC whilst staying with the club vice captain and looking for employment. A condition of his visa was that he had a return ticket home, but he hoped that he would have picked up a job before the expiry date and not have to use it. Unfortunately, the rugby club was based in the university town of Ann Arbor, and all of the part-time or low-paid jobs were taken up by students. Maybe he should have researched this a little more.

So, although enjoying his rugby enormously, he returned home happy with his experience, but jobless. He had been offered one job coaching at a sports centre, but that was to start two months in the future and with money rapidly running out he decided to use his return ticket.

Once home another really good job offer arrived, but Stu had now happily settled back into teaching at a really good school.

If only . . .

Knowing the market

Maybe if Stu had asked a few more questions before going abroad he would have realised that although his ability as a county player would give him numerous opportunities to play in the States, the possibilities of picking up employment were limited.

The USA does not have the professional set-up in rugby that we have in Europe so earning money purely through playing was not going to happen. Being paid to coach might have been a possibility, but that would have had to be with a bigger club or college. Picking up a job outside of sport might have been more realistic in another town: even more likely in another country.

Knowing your ability

This is generally quite easy. If you are playing in the national league of your sport there is a good chance that your level of performance would be welcomed in most clubs around the world.

Things take on a different perspective, though, if you can't even make the starting line-up of your *local* league team. The chances are that most countries would have numerous players of your ability, so consequently your market would be very restricted.

As already mentioned in Chapter 2, even the best team selectors make mistakes and your failure to make the team could be one of these. If you are confident this has happened, and you believe you are a better player than your playing record suggests, you are still advised to exercise some caution. Don't go to all the expense and upheaval of travelling abroad on what could become a fruitless and frustrating mission. Test yourself out in Britain by changing clubs. If you achieve more success there, then you know that your previous selectors were wrong.

The 'open' revolution

In recent years many sports have gone 'open'. In other words, sports that were ostensibly amateur now allow their players to earn money from competing.

Two prime examples of these are Rugby Union and Athletics. The opportunities in these sports for the paid employment of quality players and coaches are steadily on the increase. Advertisements for these, and many other newly professionalised sports, regularly appear in their own specialist magazines.

This is all very well for sports that advertise openly for players, but not all sports do. How, then, do you find the opportunities in sports that recruit from within their own system?

GETTING CONTACTS ABROAD

Researching

Research is absolutely vital. This was covered in Chapter 2, and the same methods for seeking opportunities in the UK can be used abroad.

When you contact a magazine ask them if they have published an article covering sport in the country of your choice. Even if clubs in these countries haven't committed money to advertising for players, they are probably still on the lookout for good talent. Write to any clubs or associations mentioned in these articles.

Sometimes tourist brochures and pocket guidebooks about your chosen country contain a section on sport. Use the same approach with these too.

Another source of useful information is newspapers, in particular the weekend editions of these. Saturday and Sunday editions, but also sometimes midweek versions, regularly contain comprehensive travel sections. Travel and holiday companies sometimes contain, often brief, sections on sport in certain countries.

Once again, the internet carries a wealth of information on opportunities abroad, with employment and sport being just two of the categories on offer.

Chapter 5 deals with accessing the internet in more detail.

Finding the openings

Using the internet is now a great way of discovering the opportunities that exist in a sport (see Chapter 5), but some sports still prefer to target their employees through specialist magazines. A past copy of *Horse and Hound* contained no fewer than 29 adverts offering employment. The jobs advertised included college lecturer, sales rep, farrier, riders and numerous grooms. Two of the opportunities were for overseas work. Chapter 10 gives contact information for many of the prominent specialist magazines.

The internet, also, contained hundreds of other opportunities to work abroad including fitness instructors in Bermuda, basketball instructors in Canada, canoeing instructors in Egypt, cycling leaders in Greece, golf instructors in Lanzarote and soccer coaches in the USA, amongst a multitude of others.

Making enquiries

If you are lucky you will know someone who has previously been to a country of interest to you and knows what the playing conditions are like. If you don't, then ask around. Somebody in your club may know a friend of a friend who can help. Finally, if your lines of enquiry dry up, put an advert on your club noticeboard, and that of any other clubs that you visit. Sportspeople are really friendly people. You will probably be amazed how much assistance you receive – even from players you considered were deadly rivals.

Using local expertise

If you are considering playing abroad you must already be playing at a reasonable level. As a result you should have some contact with your local and national coaches, or at least know their contact information. Use them. Ask them if they know of any opportunities to play abroad. They, in their years of playing and coaching, have probably made numerous contacts who might be willing to assist you in joining a foreign club.

The direct method is usually the most productive approach, but there are others.

Advertising yourself

If throughout your enquiries you can't find any openings or opportunities, try to create some for yourself.

Place an advertisement in your sport's magazine, or on the internet (see Figure 3). If you are keen to go to a particular region then contact the tourist information office for that area and enquire about advertising there. They may be able to sort out some free advertising for you, or at worst give you the addresses, and other information on their free papers and daily and evening newspapers. If you can write the advertisement in the native language this is likely to get a more positive reaction. If you can't do this you may be able to get assistance from the tourist office, one of your old school's language teachers or a friend who speaks the language.

British county-level Basketball Player, 19 years old, 1.94m tall, fluent in Spanish, is looking to compete for a club in a Spanish-speaking country during the coming season.
 Assistance with accommodation and employment would
be appreciated. If you can help please telephone 01234 567890 or write to PO Box 321, Sportown, England

Fig. 3. Sample advertisement.

Advertising precisely in this way was previously tried very successfully by two South African athletes who contacted *Athletics Weekly*. They quickly became established as members of a prominent club in the south of England.

Contacting national organisers

Again, as in Chapter 2, write to the national governing body of your sport and ask them if they can put you in touch with the national body of the country you would like to visit.

You can find the addresses of NGBs in Chapter 6.

Approaching the embassy

Another option is to write directly to the embassy of your preferred country, telling them of your intentions. Ask them for the addresses of their national associations and any other contacts they might have. It is unlikely that they would know of any opportunities that exist as they are more politically orientated – but it does no harm to ask.

The majority of embassies are based in London and their addresses can be found by looking through the London telephone directories, or again through searching the internet. Most main libraries can help with this, as they generally have these directories, but if not the librarian will probably know of alternative sources. As a last resort, because this now costs money, you could phone one of the numerous directory enquiry companies.

Trying pot luck

The least desirable option is to travel to the country of choice and seek opportunities whilst you are there.

If you decide to use this method you must plan carefully and make contingency plans for the homeward journey if your finances reach a predetermined critically low level.

This is obviously not the most recommended way of seeking a placement. A lot of the people I know who have tried this return home dejected, but have enjoyed an extended holiday abroad due to trying. Some have stayed, but ended up working in a job not connected to their sport whilst still hoping their dream will materialise. The majority, though, simply return home penniless, but normally quite happy with the experience.

If you do, however, still decide to go ahead with this option, you will have more chance of success if you are organised in the way you approach the task in hand. Focus your efforts.

Focusing your efforts

Once you arrive at your destination, focus your efforts on the locations that are most likely to yield results. Check out:

- noticeboards at sports centres;
- noticeboards at youth hostels;
- Job Centres (or their equivalent);
- the situations vacant section in the local newspaper;
- specialist newspapers like *Overseas Jobs Express*;
- noticeboards at supermarkets.

If all of the above fail then place your own advertisements in these places.

Finally, and probably most enjoyably, find the liveliest bar in town and talk to the locals, if you are competent in their language. Many, many jobs have been arranged over a friendly drink in a bar or at the local golf course or sports centre.

Relying on pot luck is the least recommended course of action as it can be very time consuming, often producing little or no results. It will almost definitely be more expensive than you imagined, and very often depressing.

However, after criticising this method, many people known to me have used this approach over the years to pick up good jobs ranging from ski resorts in Europe to hotels in the Far East.

CASE STUDY

Two Aussies strike it lucky

Whilst skiing in Les Orres in the French Alps several seasons ago I met two Australian backpackers, Luke and Jon, who came into the hotel and asked the manager if there were any temporary jobs going. Even though they were trying pot luck they had taken an intelligent approach to finding jobs. Firstly they had targeted a highly likely source of employment and secondly they made sure that they carried references with them from their most recent employers. They were working their way around Europe, staying approximately one month at a time in each resort. They started work the very next day: one in the kitchen and the other as a barman.

As expected they didn't stay long. It was rumoured that a month later they were in another hotel in Alp d'Huez.

MAKING CONTACTS ABROAD – CHECKLIST

1. Know your market – choose the right country.

2. Know your ability – are you good enough for sport in this country, or would another country provide an easier market?

3. Don't aim too high – better to work up from the bottom than receive no offers at all.

4. Research – magazines, guides, the internet, brochures, newspapers, etc., relevant to your chosen country.

5. Enquire – teammates, opponents, coaches, administrators, etc.

6. Advertise – on the internet, noticeboards, foreign and UK magazines and newspapers.

7. Contact – national organisers and embassies.

8. Pot luck – once there try sports centres, sports clubs, youth hostels, job centres, situations vacant, supermarkets and bars.

COACHING AND INSTRUCTING

If you would like to coach abroad then it would be extremely advisable, although not always absolutely necessary, to hold a

British coaching award. Many 'beginner' level awards are relatively easy to achieve and also quite inexpensive. Many Level One awards do not even require an exam to be taken at the end of the course, merely full attendance.

You can find out more about coaching awards in Chapter 7.

Why go to the expense of qualifying?

British coaching awards are generally held in high esteem abroad and are an excellent springboard in your quest for employment. They are well worth the investment. They also generally provide insurance cover for yourself, but check on this as they might not cover foreign countries.

A list of organisers of these awards is contained in Chapter 6 and there is more information on them in Chapter 7.

The same approach for gaining employment as a player can be used for coaching/instructing, so you might wish to refer to the earlier section in this chapter. In addition, you should note that many more coaches than players are now being sought through the internet. British coaches, more so than players, are in demand abroad. This is because most countries prefer to import a coach to develop their own talent rather than bring foreign players into their domestic game.

Britain typifies this approach – we often import ice hockey and basketball coaches from North America, but export soccer coaches to them.

Clubs generally work on the concept that if they import a good player he or she is still only one player. They may improve the team immediately, but a coach can develop dozens of players who will enhance their team for the long-term future.

Identifying the demand

As in the last edition good soccer, athletics and rugby coaches are in demand throughout the world, but you need to apply to the less developed countries to gain a coaching appointment in our less successful sports. Many of the posts available are through voluntary organisations which despite the name generally pay a 'wage' (see below).

The leisure industry continues to be the big, booming success story in commerce. There are numerous organisations actively seeking coaches and instructors to look after sportspeople of all ages on their activity holiday courses. Details of these companies are included in Chapter 10.

Activity holiday companies are now not only employing instructors in the traditional slot of our schools' summer holiday period, but increasingly all year round. This is due to the enormous number of family holidays that are now being taken further afield in warmer climates than found in northern Europe. The tropics and southern hemisphere are now well within reach and resorts there have been set up to cater for British and European holidaymakers. Due to this, jobs that were once considered as temporary and seasonal now provide employment all year round.

Finding work in the leisure industry

Full-time employment is often achieved by working with the same company in the northern hemisphere in our summer then after that in the southern hemisphere, in theirs. Alternatively, working in the mountains as a ski instructor in the winter, and then the same mountains during the summer leading pony trekking tours, walks or rock climbing.

By far the most common way of coaching and instructing in the leisure industry is to work the summer season on the beach as surfing/windsurf/canoe instructor, for example, and then the winter in the mountains instructing snowboarding, skiing, ice skating, etc.

There are many other permutations like this of sports that are possible to combine. Activity holiday companies are constantly advertising for instructors in:

aerobics	pony trekking	squash
archery	sailing	surfing
basketball	scuba diving	swimming
canoeing	self-defence	table tennis
climbing	skateboarding	tennis
fencing	skiing	volleyball
golf	snorkelling	waterskiing
horse riding	snowboarding	windsurfing
ice skating	soccer	yoga
paragliding		

CASE STUDY

Mike's university contacts pay dividends

Mike had a great time in Manchester, where he gained a Bachelor of Education degree, as well as taking his F.A. Coaching Award; and this is where he struck gold.

He shared a house with three other students from Didsbury College and on qualifying went on to teach at Egglescliffe School in Cleveland.

One of his housemates, however, went over to the States where he set up Summer Camps coaching the blossoming game of 'soccer' to the Americans.

When these became so successful that he needed extra experienced and qualified British coaches that he could trust, the first one he thought of was Mike.

So for two years in a row Mike coached during his school summer holidays in San Diego. Flights, accommodation and a small wage were included as part of the deal.

During the second stint, however, he struck gold. One of the local team was looking for someone to house-sit their premises while they were away on vacation, so Mike volunteered. Consequently he took his wife and kids with him on a working holiday that they will all never forget. To make it even more unforgettable, the host family even included the use of their family cars in the package.

Needless to say, all this just added up to what was an unforgettable and wonderful experience of working and sightseeing in this exotic and beautiful part of the United States.

Only other commitments stopped Mike from returning for third, fourth and fifth summers.

When I asked Mike what changes he would make if he had his time over again, he replied probably nothing; teaching had been a great career choice, but if for some reason he hadn't become a teacher, knowing what he knows now, he would have pursued a career involving skiing and would probably now be the proud owner of his own ski company.

His advice for anybody wanting to do the same sort of things as himself, is to first of all work hard to become qualified in whatever sport you are keen on and then check out the internet (or books like this) for the opportunities available.

All universities and summer camp companies in the USA advertise for soccer, and other sports, coaches every summer.

VOLUNTEERING

Most people have a misconception about voluntary work abroad because it suggests that you are working for no pay. Yet in the majority of cases this is not true. Remuneration varies greatly, from those organisations which provide nothing but food and accommodation, to others that provide these plus a wage. In general the vast majority of agencies provide pocket money on top of basic accommodation and food.

However there are some that pay a higher wage than many leisure and travel companies. Take care in your selection.

A few agencies charge a registration fee and, amazingly, also offer the lowest remuneration.

However, there are good established companies such as Voluntary Service Overseas (VSO) that look after their employees totally, even to the extent of providing expenses for buying clothes that are suitable for the region. A newer, Canadian based company called Right To Play International recruits volunteers to work throughout Africa and Asia, and pays an honorarium as well as providing ten days' training in Toronto, Canada.

Before volunteering for any project make sure you are clear about how long you want to spend in this type of work, as periods of employment can commit you to working anything from one week to three years.

There are several books in Chapter 10 that go into greater detail if you are interested in pursuing this option.

Advantages to volunteering

- ◆ Knowing that you are doing a job that is really worthwhile.
- ◆ Working in a team with definite objectives.

+ Having the opportunity to see the problems, as well as the sights, of a country at first hand.
+ All the arrangements are made for you.
+ Voluntary work always looks impressive on a CV, so is useful when applying for jobs on return to the UK.

Illustrating recent opportunities

Voluntary Service Overseas has been paying volunteers to work in sports-related projects for a long, long time. There have recently, through VSO, been opportunities to work in sport in 30 countries around the world, mainly in Asia and Africa. These positions usually require coaching, teaching and management skills as a prerequisite. Appointments vary in length from two weeks to three years and applicants must be at least 18 years old, with practically no upper age limit.

VSO do their utmost to cater for all their volunteers' requirements. All travel arrangements, including visas and work permits, are organised and paid for by them. Before leaving Britain volunteers receive a grant which adequately covers the cost of specialist clothing and equipment needed to work in the chosen country. Another grant is given halfway through the contract. VSO also cover the costs of accommodation, medical and travel insurance, and national insurance contributions. On top of all this VSO give their workers a minimum of three weeks' holiday per year and a salary. This is generally a modest living allowance paid by the employer in that country, which will not be much compared to UK rates, but is normally more than adequate to live on by local standards.

CASE STUDY

Anne is bowled over in Costa Rica

Anne went to Costa Rica as a volunteer with Cross Cultural Solutions. She loved it so much that she wrote this account:

'If I had to describe my overall experience in two words, it would be challenging and so worth it (okay that's four words!). It's been almost a month and a half since I came home, and I'm still finding it difficult to put the experience into words. Not because there isn't that much to say but because there is so much to say. I will say that it was definitely one of those experiences in which the whole is greater than the sum of its parts. There were fun parts, challenging parts, sobering parts, frustrating parts. It's so clichéd to say that this "changed my life" but I feel like it enriched my life in ways I'm still discovering. The most prominent thought in my mind as I was preparing to leave and in the days after I returned home was "I need to do this again".'

CAMP COUNSELLING AND SUMMER CAMPS

Summer camps are now common around the world, but started in North America, which is still the place that they are predominantly found. There are over 12,000 of them throughout the whole of the USA. Several holiday companies now run their own camps in various countries, but the biggest names in this field, BUNAC and Camp America, still operate mainly in the USA. Between them they offer sports-related work in:

aerobics	karate
archery	lacrosse
athletics (track and field)	life saving
baseball	motorboating
basketball	rifle shooting
camping*	rock climbing
canoeing**	rollerblading
cycling	sailing
diving	soccer
fencing	swimming
golf	tennis

gymnastics	volleyball
hiking	waterskiing
hockey	weight training
horse riding	windsurfing
judo	

*Camping offers other specialisms: outdoor cooking, campcraft and ropes courses.

**Canoeing offers other specialisms of kayaking and expeditions.

To help you with your decision-making a list of what both Camp America and BUNAC offer is included below.

- Orientation training before commencing work.
- Arranging work permits and visas.
- Return airfare and transfers to and from your camp.
- Food and accommodation.
- A basic salary.
- Six or seven weeks' holiday time, after camp, before returning to your own country.

BUNAC

BUNAC stands for British Universities North America Club and they arrange employment at summer camps in the USA and Canada. Since their inauguration in 1962 they have now branched out to arrange work in many other countries, but most of this is of the non-sporting type. More information is available on their website – details in Chapter 10.

BUNAC charge a registration fee (refundable if your application is unsuccessful), and a membership fee, if you obtain work through them. In addition you will have to pay for:

1. Travel to your interview and orientation (at a university near you).
2. Your own medical.
3. Your own visa.
4. Medical, accident and baggage insurance.

Rates of pay vary and you are advised to establish your remuneration before accepting your appointment.

Camp America

Camp America have been running summer camps for more than 30 years. They don't organise work outside the USA, but they do offer a wider range of sporting activities. Interviews are held all over the UK, so if you reach that stage you will not have too far to travel. You will not be required to undergo a medical examination, but you will have to complete a medical form. If you are given a placement you will need to get confirmation of your medical history from your doctor, who will also have to confirm your suitability for the programme. These costs are met by you. At your interview you will have to pay a first deposit, followed by a second payment if you obtain a placement. This, however, covers your visa fee and airport taxes.

The amount of 'wage' that you receive depends on your age, type of job and experience. See their website – details in Chapter 10 – for more information.

Looking at other camps around the world

Following the American example, summer camps and activity holidays have become popular in many other countries and the majority of these are organised for children. Brochures are not easy to come by as the majority of companies specialising in these holidays mail direct to schools. So ask your local P.E. teacher if they have any spare copies, as well as enquiring at your local travel agents and take your contact addresses from these. Sometimes you can find adverts for this type of holiday in national newspapers as well.

Finally, unless you have the website address of companies such as PGL, you could try a general search through one of the internet search engines like MSN, Google, etc., for summer camps – there are literally thousands of entries.

CASE STUDY

A great experience and a great holiday too!

Karen was in her second year of teacher training when some friends suggested financing a holiday in America by working in a summer camp through BUNAC.

She went through all the formalities: interview, medical, etc., before being employed as a tennis coach at Kenwood Camp in Connecticut.

After working at the summer school Karen took time out to tour around the States, taking in such attractions as the Statue of Liberty, Grand Canyon and of course Disneyland.

Karen enjoyed her time there so much that she returned to work there the following year, but this time in the higher paid job of Group Leader, which meant being responsible for 22 11-year-old children.

Only family circumstances prevented Karen from going back for a third term. She said that 'working with BUNAC has been an important part of my life. I really enjoyed the work. It also assisted in financing my tour of the States. I could not have afforded to see the Grand Canyon and other sights without it.

I am positive that having this on my CV also helped me to secure my current teaching post.'

TAKING A YEAR (OR MORE) OUT

If past experiences are borne out, most people reading this book will be either school leavers, studying at university, or just graduated, and who would like to see a bit more of the world before settling into a career.

This is not a bad idea. Many people, including future employers, think that a break from the education system not only helps you to apply yourself to future studies, but also that you will be a more mature, capable person as a result of your experiences.

Sometimes taking a year out can change your career plan and you might decide against going back to college in the immediate future. All the options listed in this book are ideal ways for you to gain employment, but the seasonal and voluntary work sections should be of particular relevance. However, if you are considering this, but would like more information, there are several books and websites on the subject listed in Chapters 5 and 10.

CASE STUDY

Simon makes a career change

Simon was nearing the end of his electrical engineering degree at Sheffield University and was considering taking a year out when his phone rang. His older sister, who was already working in Thailand, told him about an opportunity that had become available as a swimming instructor. She knew that Simon was already qualified in this area and it seemed ideal for him. Without hesitation, after term had finished Simon headed for Bangkok. He thoroughly enjoyed his work there and stayed well beyond his year out. He gained promotion and moved up to being the manager of all the hotel's leisure facilities which included tennis coaching, aerobics, weight training, etc.

He is now manager of all leisure provision within the hotel group, responsible for the whole region between Hong Kong and Thailand.

STUDYING WHILST COACHING AND COMPETING

Sports scholarships started in the USA, but have since spread to all corners of the globe. Much of the USA's sporting success was, and still is, college based. Now many other nations are trying to emulate this success by adopting the same system of offering cash incentives to the more gifted sportspeople to study at their institutions.

Although there are increasing opportunities to gain sports scholarships worldwide, the vast majority are still in American colleges – but Britain is rapidly catching up.

The National Collegiate Athletic Association (NCAA) has strict rules about when students can be signed to American college teams – so check on this before applying – the situation, however, is more relaxed in Britain.

Gaining a sports scholarship at a university has three major advantages.

1. It is a great way of playing and improving your sport.

2. Trying to compete at sport whilst holding down a full-time job often leaves you jaded and your performance suffers.

3. Once you are qualified many employers find this, plus your skill and experience, ideally suitable for their company.

Coaching opportunities

If your forte is coaching you could work within the college system by applying for a postgraduate 'assistantship'. As the title suggests you would apply to work as an assistant coach for one of the college teams and in return you receive your postgraduate tuition and accommodation free of charge. This not only enables you to come out with a higher level degree, but also gives you valuable contacts within the system which may eventually lead to further opportunities.

Most of these assistantship opportunities exist in American universities, but more and more are now appearing in the UK and other parts of the world. Traditionally, if you wanted to pursue this option, you contacted your chosen university direct. This is still viable, but now an increasing number of colleges are advertising these posts on the internet. See Chapter 6 for British universities' addresses.

Avoiding the pitfalls

If these opportunities look enticing and desirable you should heed a few words of warning. Whilst the vast majority of students returning to the UK, after completing an assisted course, recount their wonderful experiences, there have also been a small number of horror stories. Some students have returned, often without completing their course, because of the excessive pressure they were under from the college's head coach. They have complained about such things as being asked to compete whilst still injured, or to take on different roles within their sport than they are used to. For example, being accepted as a high jumper but being coerced into competing as a javelin thrower or steeplechaser to gain valuable points for their college team. Non-compliance with the coach's request is often then followed by the threat of withdrawal of the student's funding.

This is a case of 'he who pays the fiddler calls the tune' and can be understandable when the coaches themselves are under enormous pressure to produce results. However, it must be pointed out that this is not the norm. The majority of coaches conduct themselves in a totally professional manner.

The best way to avoid problems is to extensively research your preferred college, also, if finances permit, to visit it and talk to the coaching staff and students. It is worth noting, however, that you are less likely to be used as a dogsbody the more valuable you are to them. In other words the higher standard you compete at means the more likely they are to look after your welfare.

If your chosen path is to apply to American colleges then an absolutely invaluable book to consult is *Sports Scholarships and College Programs in the USA*. It comprehensively covers all aspects of sports scholarships in the States and you can find more details on it in Chapter 9.

CASE STUDY

Steven makes sacrifices to have a great time abroad
Steven missed his family and friends, fish and chips, curries and the English sense of humour, in order to pursue his dream in the USA.

He had been inspired to try for a golf scholarship when he was at a tournament in Aberystwyth and met a fellow competitor who had just completed his American degree by this method. So Steven sent his CV to several colleges. Fortunately Campbell University in North Carolina picked him up.

Steven absolutely loved it. It was hard work sometimes juggling classes and training and competing. Golf took up so much time, not like soccer where training would last a couple of hours, and competition 90 minutes. Qualifying rounds in tournaments could last five and a half hours, and training even longer.

All in all though Steven feels fortunate to have been given this opportunity to gain a qualification – he came out with a Master's Degree in Business Administration – whilst experiencing a different culture, visiting places that he'd only seen on TV, *and* improving at the sport that he loved.

For a short time Steven worked as an assistant golf coach, whilst he was studying for his Master's, but, as soon as he qualified he moved into a job that he describes as spectacular. He is now the UK Marketing Director for Disney on Ice.

He says: 'every day is different, challenging and rewarding. I get the opportunity to do some pretty spectacular things for special people. Seeing kids' excitement when they meet Mickey Mouse or their favourite Disney character is priceless.'

WORKING IN SPORTS-RELATED EMPLOYMENT

There are numerous jobs closely connected with sport that could also give rise to employment abroad. They might not involve you directly with your own sport, but the work may be satisfying merely through being associated with it. The list of British jobs contained in Chapter 2 is obviously relevant to other countries, but it does have some exceptions. For example, some of the third world countries may not be wealthy enough to employ county development officers.

Opportunities for employment in sports related jobs exist globally, but employers would expect you to have experience in your own country before applying.

If you would like to investigate this option further then refer to Chapters 2 and 5 to help you assess the market and Chapter 7 to identify the qualifications you will need.

WORKING IN CLOSE PROXIMITY TO YOUR SPORT

If you would like to work in a job that keeps you in close proximity to your sport, without actually participating – for example working in a ski resort in a domestic capacity and using your leisure time to ski – then there are countless opportunities for employment.

Leisure is the main worldwide growth industry. Experts estimate that the travel industry in Britain is growing at more than two and a half times that of GNP (gross national product).

Many leisure companies employ thousands of workers both in Britain and abroad and the internet regularly advertises opportunities for these. Apart from leisure companies, there are many other employers out there who not only advertise on the internet but also in specialist career-related magazines like *The Lady* (for domestic employment), *The Stage* (for entertainers), *Nursing Times*, etc.

Finding the right job for yourself

Holiday companies in particular require people to work as:

accounts clerk	campsite services attendant
administrative assistant	carpenter
airport rep	centre manager
babysitter	chalet maid
bar staff	chambermaid
beautician	coffee bar staff
boiler technician	cook/kitchen assistant
boat maintenance technician	courier
bus driver/staff	croupier
campsite courier	dishwasher

driver
electrician
entertainment organiser
fibre-glasser
fire safety officer
groundsman
group leader
hairdresser
handyman
holiday rep
instructor
interpreter
janitor
kindergarten teacher
manager
mechanic
musician
nanny
night auditor
nurse
office staff
painter
photographer
plumber
porter
printer
receptionist
rescue boat personnel
rodent control officer
service station staff
sewing machinist
shipping clerk
shop worker
ski lift attendant
ski lift mechanic
ski technician
store assistant
teacher
telephone operator
ticket collector
tour guide
waiter/waitress

Working for a leisure company

If you want to pursue this option make sure you apply at the right time. Most leisure companies start recruiting for their winter season between April and August. However, in the past there have still been a limited number of vacancies available in the autumn, so you could still be lucky.

Companies requiring summer workers generally accept applications between September and February, but again applicants have been successful as late as April.

Obviously, in all cases the earlier you apply the more choice you have and the greater your chances of success.

If you don't necessarily want to work in a job connected with your sport, but merely want to be close to the facilities that you need, the opportunities are endless. Many newspapers, magazines and the internet carry adverts from employers abroad asking for British men and women to work for them.

This can be a good way to earn some money and enjoy your sport, because this option has several advantages over other types of work.

- You are still fresh and keen for your sport when you have finished your daily job.
- If you have selected wisely, you are close to your sport's arena.

- You are surrounded by like-minded people.

In other categories of sports related work many people become disillusioned when they realise that they have no time or energy to participate, having spent all day coaching/teaching it.

You can find some examples of past opportunities under 'Employment in Close Proximity to Your Sport' in Chapter 5, and more ideas can be formulated from the list of journals in Chapter 10.

CASE STUDY

Ollie – what an incredible character
Ollie always wanted to be in the leisure/entertainment industry. He was German Masters Champion at table tennis in 1998 and now coaches this plus volleyball, pool and many other sports as Chief Entertainments Officer at Palm Oasis in Gran Canaria.

When I asked him what qualifications he needed for the job he replied 'None really, just a good all round ability in sport and entertaining.'

He certainly has this.

At 15 years of age he left school to study magic at college in Germany for three years. Then he went to San Francisco for a further six months advanced course. As well as these skills he also plays the guitar, piano, saxophone, flute and clarinet, and is fluent in German, English and Spanish, but says that he can only just get by in Italian and Dutch.

Ollie eventually worked his way up to this job, having first worked as a waiter in Holland, then with Eurocamp in Italy, before working in another resort in Gran Canaria.

He advises anybody wanting similar work to gain as many skills and qualifications as they can before applying, but mainly to work on their language skills.

THE ARMED FORCES

As with Britain, opportunities exist to pursue your sport whilst employed in the Armed Forces of a foreign country. It is extremely rare for a British national to do this, but there are cases of sportspeople doing so. In recent years Steve Tunstall, who was a GB cross country and track international, served his time in the French Foreign Legion.

If you are interested in pursuing this outlet you should contact the appropriate embassy. The majority of these are located in London and their details can be found in the London telephone directory (copies are normally stored at main libraries) or on the internet.

SELF-ASSESSMENT EXERCISE

1. Which option for using your sport most appeals to you?

2. Do you have the required level of skill and qualifications to enable you to use your sport?

3. Do you know who to contact to pursue your chosen option?

4. Have you decided which country you want to work in?

5. Can you speak the language?

6. Are you prepared to learn the language?

5
Finding Employment

ACCESSING THE INFORMATION

T he first edition of this book recorded that adverts for employment could be found predominantly in books, magazines, newspapers, sports clubs, sports centres and job centres, as well as on the internet. Whilst these sources are still prominent today, the internet now outstrips the others by far and has become the main source for sports employment opportunities.

Most national organising bodies now have their own website (see Chapter 6 for details) and the majority of these detail employment within their organisation. There are literally *too many* jobs to list them all in this book, so check these websites first.

The internet also contains numerous sites that detail a wealth of employment opportunities. The majority of contact information is free, but there are some agencies that charge a fee for their service. So check out the free sites first, then once these have been exhausted think about subscribing to the fee-paying sites.

Some expense, however, may be worthwhile incurring, as it could be invaluable to you. Purchase a specialist sports magazine, as this is more likely to carry employment adverts that have the most relevance to your circumstances, especially if you don't have the internet to subscribe to an ISP (internet service provider) in order to access the above mentioned wealth of adverts.

If, unfortunately, you can't afford these it is not the end of the world. Ask around your local sports club to see if you can borrow magazines from someone. If that fails, remember that some of the bigger libraries stock the most popular sports magazines in their reference section.

A list of many of the most popular sports magazines is included in Chapter 10.

Accessing the internet

The cheapest way to access the internet is to subscribe to a free ISP. However, these tend to be a lot slower than broadband, which normally incurs expense. This small expense is often worthwhile, though, as you get faster access and less sites jamming, therefore more are available. If however you don't own a computer, or have this access, ask your friends if any of them are online, or visit your local school or college and ask if you can use their facilities.

Otherwise many local libraries now offer free, or cheap, access. Other libraries charge as little as £0.75 an hour for this provision. Likewise there is now an abundance of internet cafes and cybercafes, which charge from £1 upwards. Someone in one of these institutions is normally available to show you, free of charge, how to access the sites that you need. Look them up in *Yellow Pages* and don't forget to enquire about their charges.

If you would like to be able to do more on the internet, rather than just the basics, there are numerous books, stocked by the vast majority of libraries, on this subject. There is also an abundance of free courses, mainly at your local community colleges where, of course, you will probably also be able to use the internet free of charge.

FINDING YOUR SPORT

As there is now an abundance of sports jobs advertised on the internet, you will find the majority of the information listed below comes from that source. I have had to trim this list down considerably, as I collected approximately 400% more sports vacancies than I needed for this book, and all this in just two weeks.

So only a fraction of them are detailed here, as an illustration of the types of jobs previously available, some of the exotic locations you could be working in and most importantly the addresses of the companies advertising them.

The list contains opportunities that have been recently advertised in company literature, books, magazines, newspapers or on the internet. You can find full contact addresses, telephone and fax numbers or internet details in Chapter 10. Please bear in mind that by the time you read this book the vast majority of these jobs will have been taken a long time ago, but it still may be worthwhile contacting the companies to enquire whether new opportunities have become available. Much of the work listed is seasonal, but it is often available every year, and many sportsmen and women return to work for the same company time after time.

For each opportunity listed, the internet address is given in the last column. Contact details of companies that have advertised sports related employment are also given in Chapter 10. Each sport is listed alphabetically, with employers' details, and the location of the job is detailed in the middle column.

The employment available is so varied that differing levels of qualification and experience are required. To avoid wasting your time, check on this before applying.

After the listings of jobs in sport I have also included further details of work which has recently been on offer that may not involve participating or coaching your sport, but which will give you opportunities to participate due to close proximity to it.

Finally, Chapter 10 gives details of numerous books, magazines and newspapers that contain useful information regarding finding employment through sport.

JOBS THAT HAVE RECENTLY BEEN AVAILABLE

Aerobics (fitness, yoga, pilates and dance)

Aerobics Instructor	Europe	markwarner-recruitment.co.uk
Change4Life Co-ordinator	YMCA SW London	leisureopportunities.co.uk
Dance Instructors	West London	uksport.gov.uk
Fitness/Aerobics/Dance Instructor	Ontario, Canada	campwhitepine.com
Fitness Instructors	Staines, Brighton, Southampton	gumtree.com
Fitness Instructor	Bath University	jobs.ac.uk
Fitness Centre Assistant	Lincoln	jobsite.co.uk
Full and Part Time Instructors	London	leisureopportunities.co.uk
Let Me Play Coaches (Street Dance)	London	uksport.gov.uk
NVQ Sport/fitness Assessors	All Areas of UK	totaljobs.com
Part Time Dance Teacher	1StepSports Suffolk	uksport.gov.uk
Personal Trainers	Jeddah, Saudi Arabia	www.ultraforce.co.uk
Pilates Instructor	Europe	markwarner-recruitment.co.uk
Yoga Instructor	Europe	markwarner-recruitment.co.uk

American football

Flag Coaches	Coventry Bears	bafca.com
Head Coach	Milton Keynes Pathfinders	bafca.com
Junior Contact Head Coach	Colchester Gladiators	bafca.com
Offense and Defense Coaches	Sunderland Spartans	bafca.com
Various Coaches	Bristol Aztecs	bafca.com
Various Coaches	Oxford Saints	bafca.com

STABLE TECHNICIAN (Groom)

Scale 2/3(Points 11 - 17) £13,854 - £13,823)

Applications are invited for the above post within the Museum's Estates Department.

For this interesting and unique position we are seeking someone with at least three years professional working experience with driving and riding horses and can turn out to a very high standard. Experience with working with a team of carriage horses would be an advantage. It will also be necessary to communicate with visitors and groups to the museum in a pleasant and courteous manner.

Job description, person specification and application form are available from our website or by contacting:

BEAMISH, The North of England Open Air Museum, Beamish, Co. Durham, DH9 0RG.

Tel: 0191 370 4000   Fax: 0191 370 4001

Email: office@beamish.org.uk   Website: www.beamish.org.uk

Closing date for receipt of completed applications is: 27th October, 2006
Those shortlisted only will be contacted by: 10th November, 2006

Beamish is an Equal Opportunities employer and welcomes applications from all sections of the community.
The Museum operates a No Smoking Policy

REGIONAL DEVELOPMENT OFFICER
EASTERN REGION

This temporary position is to cover maternity leave from 1 January 2007

This role requires experience of affiliated dressage and a flexible approach to working 21 hours a week from home. The successful applicant must have their own car, computer and access to email.

They will be involved in the co-ordination of affiliated competition days and venues in the region as well as developing and administering regional judge training, BYRDS activity and regional training.

Please send CV by 20 October 2006 to: Mr David Holmes, Chief Executive, British Dressage, National Agricultural Centre, Stoneleigh Park, Kenilworth, Warwickshire, CV8 2RJ Tel: 024 76 698843
Email DavidHolmes@britishdressage.co.uk

BRUSSELS BARBARIANS
Founded 1968

www.brusselsbarbarians.com

We seek new players to join us in the Belgian Championship Elite Division and enjoy life in the capital of Europe.

Possible job opportunities for new graduates in EU affairs, plus contract positions for experienced IT Consultants.

Contact: Stuart Dowsett, President
email: rugby@eurocity.be
Tel: 00 32 475 701782

Fig. 4. Examples of the sort of job advertisements you might see in magazines.

Angling and fishing

County Angling Officer	Essex	anglingtrust.net
Fishing Instructor	Ontario, Canada	campwhitepine.com

Archery

Archery Instructor	Ontario, Canada	campwhitepine.com
Archery Instructors	West London	uksport.gov.uk
Archery Instructors	Various in USA	globalchoices.co.uk
Talent Identification/Development Coach	Northern Ireland	www.sportni.net

Athletics (track and field, cross-country)

Apprentice Coach Combined Events	Lee Valley, London	uka.org.uk
Apprentice Coach Paralympic Team	Lee Valley, London	uka.org.uk
Athletics Coaches	West London	uksport.gov.uk
National Development Officer	CP Sport Nottingham	uksport.gov.uk
National Event Coach Pole Vault	Loughborough	uksport.gov.uk
UK Coaching and Development Co-ordinator	Solihull	uksport.gov.uk

Badminton

After School Coach	Reading, Berks	uksport.gov.uk
BadmintonEngland Regional Manager	South West	leisureopportunities.co.uk
Edge Hill University Head Coach	Ormskirk, Lancashire	uksport.gov.uk
Volunteers for World Champs 2011	London	uksport.gov.uk

Baseball, softball and rounders

After School Rounders Coach	Reading, Berks	uksport.gov.uk
Baseball Instructor	Ontario, Canada	campwhitepine.com
Operations Assistant	BSUK, London	uksport.gov.uk
Regional Rounders Officer	West Midlands	uksport.gov.uk

Basketball

After School Coach	Reading, Berkshire	uksport.gov.uk
Basketball Instructor	Ontario, Canada	campwhitepine.com
BB Scotland Player Pathway Manager	Edinburgh	uksport.gov.uk
Edge Hill University Men's Head Coach	Ormskirk, Lancashire	uksport.gov.uk

Edge Hill University Women's Head

Coach	Ormskirk, Lancashire	uksport.gov.uk
Let Me Play BB Coaches	West London	uksport.gov.uk
Let Me Play Coaches	London	uksport.gov.uk
Schools and Community BB Coach	Spalding, Lincolnshire	uksport.gov.uk
Strength and Conditioning Intern	Bristol Academy of Sport	uksport.gov.uk
Wheelchair BB Development Officer	Loughborough	uksport.gov.uk

Boxing

Boxing Coach	West London	uksport.gov.uk
Boxing Development Manager	Kent	uksport.gov.uk
County Development Officer	Essex and ABA	uksport.gov.uk

Camping

Backroads	Worldwide	www.backroads.com
Canvas Holidays	Throughout Europe	canvasholidays.co.uk
Montage/Demontage Assistants	Across Europe	holidaybreakjobs.com
Outdoor Recreation Instructor	Ontario, Canada	campwhitepine.com
Pioneering and Outdoor Living	Various across USA	globalchoices.co.uk

Canoeing and kayaking

BCU Instructors	Derbyshire	www.rya.org.uk
BCU Instructors	Ringwood, New Forest	www.rya.org.uk
Canoe/Kayak Instructor	Ontario, Canada	campwhitepine.com
Canoeing Instructors	Various in USA	globalchoices.co.uk
Junior Slalom Development Coach	Canoe England	uksport.gov.uk
Kayak Instructors	Isles of Scilly	www.rya.org.uk
Kayaking Instructors	Teignmouth	www.rya.org.uk
Watersports Instructors	UK, France and Spain	www.pgl.co.uk
Watersports Instructors	France	www.clubmedjobs.com

Climbing (see rock climbing and abseiling)

Cricket

After School Coach	Reading, Berkshire	uksport.gov.uk
Cricket Development Coach	Wyre, Lancashire	www.ecb.co.uk
Edge Hill University Head Coach	Ormskirk, Lancashire	uksport.gov.uk

| Performance Administrator | Derbyshire | www.ecb.co.uk |

Curling

| Head Coaches (Men, Women, Wheelchair) | Scotland | uksport.gov.uk |
| Performance Director | Scotland | sportscotland.org.uk |

Cycling (including BMX and mountain biking)

Backroads	Worldwide	www.backroads.com
Bicycle Couriers	Across Europe	holidaybreakjobs.com
BMX Instructor	Europe	www.clubmedjobs.com
Major Events and Projects Manager	B. Cycling Manchester	uksport.gov.uk
Mountain Biking Instructor	Ontario, Canada	campwhitepine.com
Mountain Biking Instructors	Various across USA	globalchoices.co.uk
Smoothie Bike Instructor	Birmingham	uksport.gov.uk

Diving (includes scuba and snorkelling)

| Watersports Instructors | UK, France and Spain | www.pgl.co.uk |
| Watersports Instructors | France | www.clubmedjobs.com |

Equestrianism

Apprentice Groom	Berkshire	www.bhs.org.uk
Development Officer	Yorkshire	www.bhs.org.uk
Experienced Grooms	West Yorkshire and Berkshire	www.bhs.org.uk
Full Time Yard Groom	Surrey	www.bhs.org.uk
Gap Year Placement	Wiltshire	www.bhs.org.uk
Horse Riding Instructor	Ontario, Canada	campwhitepine.com
Horse Riding Instructors	Various in USA	globalchoices.co.uk
Instructors	Berkshire and Somerset	www.bhs.org.uk
Instructors	Bermuda and Canada	www.bhs.org.uk
Instructors	Hong Kong and Australia	www.bhs.org.uk
Instructors	London and Suffolk	www.bhs.org.uk
Instructors	Spain and Dubai	www.bhs.org.uk

Fencing

| Media Officer/Partner | Home Based | uksport.gov.uk |

Football (see American football, Aussie Rules, Gaelic football, soccer, etc.)

Golf

Director of Golf	Pravets Golf and Spa, Bulgaria	pga.info
Director of Golf	Lan Hai Golf Club, Shanghai	pga.info
Golf Club Secretary	Pontypridd, Wales	fish4jobs.co.uk
Golf Operations	Scottish Golf Union	pga.info
Golf Operations	Jumeirah Estates, Dubai	pga.info
Golf Services	The Golf Foundation	pga.info
Head Professional	Sonning Golf Club	pga.info
Head Professional	Newark Golf Club	pga.info
Little Golfers Coaches	Kent, Surrey, Hants	uksport.gov.uk
National and Regional Coaches	Scottish Golf Union	pga.info
Qualified Professional	Golf Made Simple	pga.info
Qualified Professional	Crondon Park Academy	pga.info
Qualified Professional	Tickenham Golf Club	pga.info
Qualified Professional	Abbotsley Golf Club	pga.info
Qualified Professional	S. Herefordshire Golf Club	pga.info
Qualified Professional	Thamesview Golf Centre	pga.info
Regional Development Officer	Nationwide	leisureopportunities.co.uk
Strength and Conditioning Intern	Bristol Academy of Sport	uksport.gov.uk
Training Applicant/Reg. Assistant	Waterford Golf Club	pga.info
Training Applicant/Reg. Assistant	Sand Moor Golf Club	pga.info
Training Applicant/Reg. Assistant	The Ridge Golf Club	pga.info
Training Applicant/Reg. Assistant	Sutton Green Golf Club	pga.info

Gymnastics

After School Coach	Reading, Berkshire	uksport.gov.uk
County Development Officer	Merseyside	uksport.gov.uk
Gymnastics Coach	Bristol	uksport.gov.uk
Gymnastics Coaches	Various in USA	globalchoices.co.uk
Let Me Play Coaches	London	uksport.gov.uk
Level 2/3 Coaches	Across Kent	uksport.gov.uk
Part Time Teacher 1StepSports	Suffolk	uksport.gov.uk
Tumble Tots Couriers	Across Europe	holidaybreakjobs.com

Women's Beam and Artistic National Coach	Lilleshall	sports-council-wales.org.uk
Women's National Junior Coach	Lilleshall	sports-council-wales.org.uk

Hiking (see walking)

Hockey (field hockey)

After School Coach	Reading, Berkshire	uksport.gov.uk
After School Coach	Hadleigh, Ipswich	englandhockey.co.uk
City University Coach	London	englandhockey.co.uk
Edge Hill University Men's Head Coach	Ormskirk, Lancashire	uksport.gov.uk
Edge Hill University Women's Head Coach	Ormskirk, Lancashire	uksport.gov.uk
Head and Assistant Coaches	Wolverhampton	englandhockey.co.uk
John Moores Uni.Men's Head Coach	Liverpool	uksport.gov.uk
Ladies 1st XI Coach	Yately, Hampshire	englandhockey.co.uk
Level 2 (or above) Coach	Bromsgrove Schools	englandhockey.co.uk

Horse riding (see equestrianism)

Ice hockey and ice skating

Ice Stewards	Chester UK	fish4jobs.co.uk
In Line Hockey Instructor	Ontario, Canada	campwhitepine.com

Judo and karate (see self defence)

Kayaking (see canoeing)

Netball

Development Officer	Nottingham	uksport.gov.uk
Edge Hill University Assistant Coach	Ormskirk, Lancashire	uksport.gov.uk
Officiating Manager	Flex.work, Hitchin base	uksport.gov.uk

Orienteering

Outdoor Recreation Instructor	Ontario, Canada	campwhitepine.com

Rafting (see canoeing or sailing)

Rock climbing, ropes and abseiling

Rock Climbing and Ropes Instructors	Various across USA	globalchoices.co.uk
Rock Climbing Instructor	Ontario, Canada	campwhitepine.com

Rowing

Adaptive Rowing Coach	Wales	britishrowing.org
British R. Online Projects Officer	Hammersmith, London	uksport.gov.uk
Community Coach	Newcastle	britishrowing.org
Community Coach	Warrington RC	britishrowing.org
Explore Rowing Activity Co-ordinator	London	britishrowing.org
Girl's Head Coach	Surbiton High School	britishrowing.org
Head Coach	Lancaster University	britishrowing.org
Head Coach	Birmingham University	britishrowing.org
Head Coach	University of the West of England, Bristol	britishrowing.org
Head Performance Coach	Cambridge	uksport.gov.uk
High Performance Coach	Henley RC	britishrowing.org
High Performance Coach	Loughborough University	uksport.gov.uk
Rowing Coach	Liverpool	britishrowing.org
Rowing Development Officer	Southampton	britishrowing.org
Sports Administrator	London	britishrowing.org
Women's Head Coach	Cambridge University	britishrowing.org

Rugby League

Commercial Manager	Wakefield T. Wildcats	uksport.gov.uk
Edge Hill University Men's Head Coach	Ormskirk, Lancashire	uksport.gov.uk
Edge Hill University Men's Asst. Coach	Ormskirk, Lancashire	uksport.gov.uk
Education and Training Specialist	Leeds	uksport.gov.uk
Strength and Cond. Internship	Bradford Bulls	uksport.gov.uk

Rugby Union

After School Coach	Reading, Berkshire	uksport.gov.uk
Child Protection Administrator	Welsh RFU, Cardiff	uksport.gov.uk
Community Rugby Coach	Harlequins, South East	uksport.gov.uk
Community Rugby Coach	North Herefordshire	www.rfu.com

Community Rugby Coaches	Various across England	www.rfu.com
Community Rugby Coaches	Oldham and Nottingham	uksport.gov.uk
Development Officer	Surrey/London	uksport.gov.uk
Edge Hill University Men's Head Coach	Ormskirk, Lancashire	uksport.gov.uk
Fitness Coach England Saxons	Throughout England	uksport.gov.uk
Referee Performance and Development	Welsh RFU Centre of Excellence	uksport.gov.uk
Regional Development Manager	Welsh RFU Ospreys Area	uksport.gov.uk
Regional Rugby Manager	East Midlands	uksport.gov.uk
Rugerbeez Children's Head Coach	Wimbledon and Guildford	uksport.gov.uk
Rugbytots Coaches	Various in south UK	uksport.gov.uk
Strength and Conditioning Intern	Bristol Academy of Sport	uksport.gov.uk
Women's Assistant Coach	Loughborough	uksport.gov.uk
Women's Divisional Coaches	Various UK Locations	uksport.gov.uk
Women's Divisional Squad Managers	Various UK Locations	uksport.gov.uk
Women's Team Coaches	Saracens London	uksport.gov.uk

Sailing

Academy Director	Oman	www.rya.org.uk
Assistant Marine Manager	Jeddah, Saudi Arabia	ultraforce.co.uk
Chief Instructor	Eastbourne	www.rya.org.uk
Dinghy and Powerboat Instructors	Ringwood, New Forest	www.rya.org.uk
Dinghy Instructors	Poole	www.rya.org.uk
Dinghy Instructors	Europe	markwarner-recruitment.co.uk
Keelboat Instructors	Brighton	www.rya.org.uk
Marina Manager	Bahrain, Arabian Coast	ultraforce.co.uk
Marina Operations Managers	Europe and the Gulf	ultraforce.co.uk
Part Time and Freelance Instructors	Milton Keynes	www.rya.org.uk
Race Skipper/Instructor	On the high seas	www.rya.org.uk
Regional Club Racing Coaches	Nationwide	www.rya.org.uk
RYA and BCU Instructors	Derbyshire	www.rya.org.uk
RYA Coaching Development Manager	Southampton based	uksport.gov.uk
RYA Instructor	Langstone, Hampshire	www.rya.org.uk
RYA Instructors	London	www.rya.org.uk
RYA Instructors	France and UK	www.rya.org.uk
Sailing and Powerboat Instructors	Isles of Scilly	www.rya.org.uk
Sailing Instructor	Ontario, Canada	campwhitepine.com

Sailing Instructors	Teignmouth	www.rya.org.uk
Sailing Instructors	Various in USA	globalchoices.co.uk
Skippers, Engineers and Hosts	UK and Worldwide	sunsail.co.uk
Watersports Instructors	UK, France and Spain	www.pgl.co.uk

Self defence (judo, karate, wrestling, etc.)

Full and Part Time Judo Coaches	Linkai Club, Thames Valley	britishjudo.org.uk
Martial Arts Instructors	Various across USA	globalchoices.co.uk
Martial Arts Instructors	West London	uksport.gov.uk

Snowsports (skiing, snowboarding, etc.)

Scottish Snowsports Co-ordinator	Edinburgh	uksport.gov.uk
Ski and Snowboard Hosts	Europe	markwarner-recruitment.co.uk
Ski and Snowboard Instructors	Throughout Europe	halsbury.com
Ski and Snowboard Instructors	Europe	ski-jobs.co.uk
Ski Hosts and Ski Reps	Europe	ski-jobs.co.uk
Ski Rep Crystal Holidays	Alpine Country	jobsinwinter.co.uk
Ski Reps	France and Spain	www.pgl.co.uk
Ski Reps	Throughout Europe	halsbury.com
Ski Technician	Europe	ski-jobs.co.uk

Soccer (as opposed to American football, Aussie Rules, etc.)

After School Coach	Reading, Berkshire	uksport.gov.uk
After School Coaches	Across N. Ireland	henrysport.co.uk
Children's Football Coach	Various around London	uksport.gov.uk
Director of Football	University of St Andrews	uksport.gov.uk
Doping Control Programme Officer	F.A. Wembley	uksport.gov.uk
Football Coaches	Across the USA	www.ukelite.com
Football Coaches	Overseas	tuitraveljobs.co.uk
Football Coaches	Europe	markwarner-recruitment.co.uk
Football Development Officer	Haverhill, Sussex	uksport.gov.uk
Football Development Officer	University of Bath	uksport.gov.uk
Get into Football Officers	Nationwide	www.thefa.com
Get into Football Officer	Salford	www.leisurejobs.com
Let Me Play Coaches	London	uksport.gov.uk

Middlesbro' College Soccer Coach	Cleveland, UK	eteach.com
Sat. am. and School Holidays Coaches	Southampton	southampton.gumtree.com
Soccer Coaches	New York Red Bulls	redbullsacademy.com
Soccer Coaches	West London	uksport.gov.uk
Soccer Instructor	Ontario, Canada	ampwhitepine.com

Squash (and racquetball)

Coach and Club Steward	Prestbury	englandsquashandracketball.com
Development Coach	Durham	englandsquashandracketball.com
Development Coach	West Midlands	englandsquashandracketball.com
High Performance Coach	Manchester	englandsquashandracketball.com
National Coach	Manchester	uksport.gov.uk
Regional Coaches	All across UK	englandsquashandracketball.com
Regional Manager – South	South of England	uksport.gov.uk
Squash Coach – David Lloyd's	Cheshire	englandsquashandracketball.com
Squash Coaches	West London	uksport.gov.uk

Surfing and wakeboarding

Surf Coach	Bournemouth	www.britsurf.co.uk
Surf Coach	Bundoran	www.britsurf.co.uk
Surf Coach	Newquay	www.britsurf.co.uk
Surf Coaches	Bude	www.britsurf.co.uk
Surf Instructor	Bantham Academy	www.britsurf.co.uk
Surf Instructor	Costa Rica	www.britsurf.co.uk
Surf Instructor	Sri Lanka	www.britsurf.co.uk
Wakeboarding Instructor	Ontario, Canada	campwhitepine.com
Watersports Instructors	UK, France and Spain	www.pgl.co.uk

Swimming and lifesaving

Assistant Coach	Epsom DSC	swimming.org
Assistant Coach	City of Cambridge	swimming.org
ASA Trainee Aquatic Assistants	Various Locations	uksport.gov.uk
Club Coach	Farnham ASC	swimming.org
Club Coach	Chalfont Otters	swimming.org
Club Coach	Wombourne SC	swimming.org
Edge Hill Uni. Head Coach	Ormskirk, Lancashire	uksport.gov.uk

Head Coach	Ledbury ASC	swimming.org
Head Coach	Alton and District SC	swimming.org
Lifeguards and Instructors	Various across USA	globalchoices.co.uk
Lifeguard Trainers/Assessors	Saudi Arabia	ultraforce.co.uk
Mini Swimming Couriers	Across Europe	holidaybreakjobs.com
Pool Attendants	Europe	markwarner-recruitment.co.uk
Schools Swimming Teachers	Wolverhampton	swimming.org
Squad Coach	Bournemouth Dolphins	swimming.org
Swimming Instructor	Ontario, Canada	campwhitepine.com
Swimming Instructors	Overseas	tuitraveljobs.co.uk
Swimming Teachers	Bristol and Bath	uksport.gov.uk

Table tennis

Club Support and Coaching Officer	North East England	uksport.gov.uk
Edge Hill University Head Coach	Ormskirk, Lancashire	uksport.gov.uk
Event Management Disabled Champs	English Institute, Sheffield	uksport.gov.uk
Regional Coach	Eastern Region	uksport.gov.uk

Ten Pin Bowling

Junior Inter Counties Secretary	Ten Pin Bowling HQ, Essex	btba.org.uk

Tennis

Community Tennis Coach	Telford & Wrekin	lta.org.uk
Disability Tennis Development Manager	Scotland	uksport.gov.uk
Head Coach, Westway Sports Centre	Middlesex	lta.org.uk
ITF Coaching Assistant	Roehampton, SW London	uksport.gov.uk
Male and Female Coaches	Saudi Arabia and Gulf	ultraforce.co.uk
National Talent Performance Manager	Wales	sports-council-wales.org.uk
Performance Coach, Connaught Club	Essex	lta.org.uk
Tennis Coach at Dulwich College	London	uksport.gov.uk
Tennis Coaches at David Lloyd's	Aberdeen, Ipswich and York	lta.org.uk
Tennis Coaches West	London	uksport.gov.uk
Tennis Development Officer	London Boroughs	uksport.gov.uk
Tennis Coaches	Europe	markwarner-recruitment.co.uk
Tennis Coaches	US and Worldwide	pbitennis.com

| Tennis Instructor | Ontario, Canada | campwhitepine.com |
| Tennis Instructors | Various across USA | globalchoices.co.uk |

Triathlon

| Membership Co-ordinator | British Triathlon Federation, Loughborough | uksport.gov.uk |
| Regional Programme Manager | South East England | uksport.gov.uk |

Volleyball

Beach Volleyball Instructor	Ontario, Canada	campwhitepine.com
Director of Sport/Volleyball	Fresno, California	summerjobs.com
Edge Hill University Head Coach	Ormskirk, Lancashire	uksport.gov.uk
Let Me Play VB Coaches	West London	uksport.gov.uk
National Academy Head Coach	Loughborough College	uksport.gov.uk

Walking (hiking and rambling)

Backroads	Worldwide	www.backroads.com
Leaders	UK and Abroad	ramblersholidays.co.uk
Walking Guides	Europe	crystalholidays.co.uk

Waterskiing

| Water Skiing Instructor | Europe | markwarner-recruitment.co.uk |
| Water Skiing/Wakeboard Instructors | Maine, USA | camplaurel.com |

Windsurfing (and kite surfing)

Head Instructor	Europe	markwarner-recruitment.co.uk
Kite Surfing Instructor	Europe	markwarner-recruitment.co.uk
Watersports Instructor	France	www.clubmedjobs.com
Watersports Instructors	UK, France and Spain	www.pgl.co.uk
Windsurf Instructors	Isles of Scilly	www.rya.org.uk
Windsurfing Instructor	Europe	markwarner-recruitment.co.uk
Windsurfing Instructor	Ontario, Canada	campwhitepine.com
Windsurfing Instructors	Teignmouth	www.rya.org.uk

Multi sports and general activities

| Active Communities Coaches | Ballymena, Northern Ireland | www.sportni.net |
| Activities Instructors | Ontario, Canada | campwhitepine.com |

Activity Instructors	UK, France and Spain	www.pgl.co.uk
After School Dodgeball Coach	Reading, Berkshire	uksport.gov.uk
Disability Sport Development Officer	Doncaster Rovers	uksport.gov.uk
Let Me Play Coaches	London	uksport.gov.uk
Multi Sports Coaches	Reading	uksport.gov.uk
Schools Sports Coaches	Richmond and Twickenham	totaljobs.com
School Sport Competition Manager	Cambridge Area	uksport.gov.uk
Schools Multi Skills Coach	Spalding, Lincolnshire	uksport.gov.uk
Sport and Recreation Supervisor	University of Ulster	indeed.com
Sports Activities Co-ordinator	Oman, Middle East	ultraforce.co.uk
Sports Coaches for Holiday Season	Spain and Canary Islands	ultraforce.co.uk
Waterfront Manager	Europe	markwarner-recruitment.co.uk
Watersports Instructors	France	www.clubmedjobs.com

EMPLOYMENT IN CLOSE PROXIMITY TO YOUR SPORT

Accounting (auditing)

Accountant	Europe	markwarner-recruitment.co.uk
Finance and Administration Officer	Cardiff	
Welsh Badminton		uksport.gov.uk
Finance Supervisor	Manchester	britishcycling.org.uk
Hotel Accountant	Europe	ski-jobs.co.uk

Activity organiser and entertainers

Group Leaders	UK, France and Spain	www.pgl.co.uk
Holiday Advisor	Overseas	tuitraveljobs.co.uk
Sport Tour Operator	Kingston upon Thames	uksport.gov.uk
Trip Operations Support Specialist	Berkeley, California	www.backroads.com

Administration

Administrators	UK, France and Spain	www.pgl.co.uk
Commercial Solicitor	Wembley	www.thefa.com
Corporate Sport Sales Executive	London	jobsite.co.uk
County Tennis Administrators	Kent and Derbyshire	www.lta.org.uk
Executive Director Tennis F.	London	uksport.gov.uk

Litigation Solicitor	Wembley	www.thefa.com
Marketing Director English Snooker	Frimley Surrey	englishsnooker.com
Overseas Recruitment Assistant	Northwich UK	eurocamp.co.uk
ProCycling Magazine Editor	Bath	totaljobs.com
PR Executive	Sport!London	totaljobs.com
Sailing Centre Administrator	Isles of Scilly	www.rya.org.uk
Sales Consultant Coventry City FC	Coventry	uksport.gov.uk
Support Staff	Ontario, Canada	campwhitepine.com
Ticket Office Administrator	Twickenham	www.rfu.com

Barstaff

Bar and Dining Room Staff	Europe	markwarner-recruitment.co.uk
Bar Hosts Crystal Holidays	3 Alpine Countries	jobsinwinter.co.uk
Barmen and Waiters	France	www.clubmedjobs.com
Bar Staff	Australia & Canada	globalchoices.co.uk
Bar Staff	Europe	ski-jobs.co.uk
Bar Supervisors Crystal Holidays	3 Alpine Countries	jobsinwinter.co.uk
Chalet Chef Crystal Holidays	Alpine Country	jobsinwinter.co.uk

Catering

Breakfast and Commis Chefs	Europe	markwarner-recruitment.co.uk
Butchers and Bakers	France	www.clubmedjobs.com
Catering Assistants	UK, France & Spain	www.pgl.co.uk
Chalet Chefs – Ski Power	Courchevel, France	goodskiguide.com
Chalet Chef – Snow	Retreat La Tania, France	goodskiguide.com
Chefs	UK, France and Spain	www.pgl.co.uk
Chefs	France	www.clubmedjobs.com
Chef de Partie Crystal Holidays	Alpine Country	jobsinwinter.co.uk
Chef de Partie and Sous Chefs	Europe	markwarner-recruitment.co.uk
Commis Chef Crystal Holidays	Alpine Country	jobsinwinter.co.uk
Culinary	Singapore	globalchoices.co.uk
Dining Room Staff	Ontario, Canada	campwhitepine.com
Dishwashers and Storekeepers	France	www.clubmedjobs.com
Gen. Catering Manager Premier Football Club	London	caterersearch.com
Head Chef Crystal Holidays	Alpine Country	jobsinwinter.co.uk

Hotel Chefs – Ski Power	Val d'Isere, France	goodskiguide.com
Kitchen Porter/Night Porter	Alpine Country	jobsinwinter.co.uk
Restaurant Supervisor Crystal Holidays	Alpine Country	jobsinwinter.co.uk
Restaurant Workers	Greek Islands	globalchoices.co.uk
Sous Chef Crystal Holidays	Alpine Country	jobsinwinter.co.uk
Waiters and Waitresses	Australia and Canada	globalchoices.co.uk

Cheerleaders, dancers and entertainers

Entertainers	Overseas	tuitraveljobs.co.uk
Entertainment Trainee	Singapore	globalchoices.co.uk
Let Me Play Coaches (cheerleading)	London	uksport.gov.uk
Singers	Egypt and Tenerife	thestage.co.uk

Childcare and child protection

Cabin Counsellors	Ontario, Canada	campwhitepine.com
Childcare Staff	Europe	ski-jobs.co.uk
Childcare Supervisor Crystal Hols	Alpine Country	jobsinwinter.co.uk
Children's Activities Leader	Europe	markwarner-recruitment.co.uk
Children's Couriers Across	Europe	holidaybreakjobs.com
Children's Rep	Overseas	tuitraveljobs.co.uk
Children's Rep	France	www.clubmedjobs.com
Nannies	Europe	markwarner-recruitment.co.uk
Nannies and Private Nannies		
Crystal Hols	Alpine Countries	jobsinwinter.co.uk
NSPCC Senior Consultant	Leicestershire and UK	uksport.gov.uk
Nanny/Au Pair – Ski Hiver	Les Arcs, France	goodskiguide.com
Whizz Kids Leaders Crystal Hols	Alpine Countries	jobsinwinter.co.uk

Computing and audio visual

BritishGymnastics AudioVisual Technician	Nationwide	uksport.gov.uk
IT Internship	Canada	globalchoices.co.uk

Driving

Driver/Maintenance	Europe	markwarner-recruitment.co.uk
Drivers	UK, France and Spain	www.pgl.co.uk
Drivers	Europe	ski-jobs.co.uk

| Drivers | Europe | crystalholidays.co.uk |

Gap year jobs

Multitude of different Jobs	Worldwide	globalchoices.co.uk
Multitude of different Jobs	Worldwide	bunac.org.uk
Multitude of different Jobs	Worldwide	campamerica.co.uk

Health and beauty

Aestheticians	Banff, Canada	fairmontcareers.com
Beauty Therapists	Europe	markwarner-recruitment.co.uk
Hairdressers	Europe	markwarner-recruitment.co.uk
Health Spa Trainee	Singapore	globalchoices.co.uk

Hotel and chalet staff

Chalet Chef Couple – Ski Power	La Tania, France	goodskiguide.com
Chalet Couple – Ski Dazzle	La Tania, France	goodskiguide.com
Chalet Host Crystal Holidays	Alpine Country	jobsinwinter.co.uk
Chalet Supervisor Crystal Holidays	Alpine Country	jobsinwinter.co.uk
Hotel Workers	Greek Islands	globalchoices.co.uk
Hotel Workers	Australia and Canada	globalchoices.co.uk
Housekeeping Assistants	UK, France and Spain	www.pgl.co.uk
Housekeeper Supervisor Crystal Hols.	Alpine Country	jobsinwinter.co.uk

Hospitality and tourism

| Hospitality Trainee | Singapore | globalchoices.co.uk |
| Internship in H & T | Canada | globalchoices.co.uk |

Maintenance and stock

Bicycle Mechanic	Salt Lake City, USA	www.backroads.com
Fitness Equipment Engineer	West/Nationwide	leisureopportunities.co.uk
Handyman Crystal Holidays	Alpine Country	jobsinwinter.co.uk
Maintenance Staff	Europe	crystalholidays.co.uk
Maintenance Staff	Ontario, Canada	campwhitepine.com
Repair and Maintenance Engineers	Across Europe	holidaybreakjobs.com
Warehouse Administrator	Across Europe	holidaybreakjobs.com

Management

Active Skills Web Manager	London	uksport.gov.uk
Activities Manager	Europe	markwarner-recruitment.co.uk
Area Manager Crystal Holidays	France	jobsinwinter.co.uk
Asst. Hotel Manager Crystal Holidays	Alpine Country	jobsinwinter.co.uk
Centre Managers	Hungerford, Berkshire and Crowborough	leisureopportunities.co.uk
Customer Service Manager Crystal Holidays	Alpine Country	jobsinwinter.co.uk
Duty Manager	Somerset	leisureopportunities.co.uk
Fitness Manager	Borehamwood	leisureopportunities.co.uk
Fitness/Sports Centre Managers	Delhi and Hyderabad, India	ultraforce.co.uk
General Leisure Manager	North Yorks	leisureopportunities.co.uk
Health Club Managers	Across Europe	leisureopportunities.co.uk
Hotel Manager Crystal Holidays	Alpine country	jobsinwinter.co.uk
Hotel Manager	Europe	markwarner-recruitment.co.uk
Leisure Club Manager	Accrington	leisureopportunities.co.uk
Racquets Manager	Bracknell	www.lta.org.uk
Restaurant Manager Crystal Holidays	Alpine country	jobsinwinter.co.uk
Salon Manager	Europe	markwarner-recruitment.co.uk
Sports Centre Duty Manager	Royal Holloway University	leisureopportunities.co.uk
Student Activities Manager	Salford University	salfordstudents.com
Technical Operations Manager (Olympics)	London	theladders.co.uk
Tennis Club Manager	Cheltenham	www.lta.org.uk
Tennis Manager	Europe	markwarner-recruitment.co.uk

Medical and first aid

First Aid and CPR Officers	Various in USA	globalchoices.co.uk
First Aid Officer	Europe	markwarner-recruitment.co.uk
Nurses	Ontario, Canada	campwhitepine.com
Recreation Health and Safety Officer	Jeddah, Saudi Arabia	sportsjobs.net

Office staff

British Rowing Admin. Assistant	London	britishrowing.org

Customer Service Staff	Europe	ski-jobs.co.uk
Office Co-ordinator	BPA, London	uksport.gov.uk
PA to Chairman and CEO	British Equestrian Federation	sports-council-wales.org.uk
Receptionists	Ross-on-Wye	www.pgl.co.uk

Physiotherapy (sports therapy and massage)

England Cricket Team	Loughborough	uksport.gov.uk
Head Academy Physio	Hull RFC	uksport.gov.uk
Head Physio UK Athletics	National	uka.org.uk
Leeds Metropolitan University	Leeds	uksport.gov.uk
Long Term Athlete Development	Northampton Saints RFC	uksport.gov.uk
Luton Town FC	Luton	uksport.gov.uk
Notts County Youth Team	Nottingham	uksport.gov.uk
RFUW Divisional Squad Physios	Various Locations	www.rfu.com
Senior Paralympic Physio	UK Athletics	uka.org.uk
Senior Physio – GB Rowing	Bisham Abbey, Buckinghamshire	uksport.gov.uk
SportScotland/Swimming	Stirling	uksport.gov.uk
Sports Massage Therapists	Europe	markwarner-recruitment.co.uk
Sports Therapists	Milton Keynes and London	uksports.gov.uk

Sales staff

| Retail Associate | Singapore | globalchoices.co.uk |
| Supermarket Staff | Canada | globalchoices.co.uk |

Sports development (co-ordination, performance, etc.)

Active Schools Co-ordinators	Oban and Isle of Bute	totaljobs.com
Director of Sport, Bishop Burton College	Beverley, Yorkshire	leisureopportunities.co.uk
Exercise Physiologist	SportScotland	uksport.gov.uk
Football Development Officer	Gloucester FA	www.thefa.com
Get into Football Officers	Numerous across UK	www.thefa.com
Gymnastics Centre Co-ordinator	Nottingham	uksport.gov.uk
Senior Sports Development Officer	Hartlepool	leisureopportunities.co.uk

Sport and Exercise Science Support Officer	University of Brighton	uksport.gov.uk
Sports Development Manager	Daventry	leisureopportunities.co.uk
Sports Development Officer	Daventry	leisureopportunities.co.uk
Sports Leader Foundation Managers	West Midlands	leisureopportunities.co.uk
Sports Performance Manager	New Zealand	totaljobs.com
Talent and Performance Co-ordinator	Kent	www.lta.org.uk

Teaching and lecturing

English, French or German Teachers	Spain	globalchoices.co.uk
English Teachers	Brazil and China	globalchoices.co.uk
Lecturer in Sport	Hartlepool	totaljobs.com
Lecturer in Sports Therapy	Newcastle	totaljobs.com
Male and Female P.E. Teachers	Various across UK	totaljobs.com
Senior Sports Studies Lecturer	University of Herts	uksport.gov.uk
Trainee Sport Lecturer	Central Sussex College	workthing.com

6
Making Contact

This chapter lists the addresses, telephone numbers and websites of most of the major UK sports governing bodies. It was accurate when going to press, however it is constantly changing with additions, deletions, changes of address, telephone numbers, etc. So if you cannot find your association here, or cannot access them through the data given, contact the information centre at one of the national governing bodies listed below or contact your local library for information.

If you require a sport that is not listed then either contact UK Sport (uksport.gov.uk), 40 Bernard Street, London WC1N 1ST, tel: (020) 7211 5100 for advice, or else enter the name of your sport into one of the internet search engines (MSN, Google, Bing, Lycos, etc.) on a computer.

CONTACTING YOUR NATIONAL GOVERNING BODY

Sport England, 3rd Floor, Victoria House, Bloomsbury Square, London WC1B 4SE. Tel: 08458 508508. www.sportengland.org

Sport for Northern Ireland, Upper Malone Road, Belfast BT9 5LA. Tel: 028 90 381222. www.sportni.net

Sport Scotland, Caledonia House, South Gyle, Edinburgh EH12 9DQ. Tel: (0131) 317 7200. www.sportscotland.org.uk

Sports Council for Wales, Sophia Gardens, Cardiff CF11 9SW. Tel: 0845 045 0904. www.sports-council-wales.org.uk

Contacting your sport's national governing body

Aerobics and Fitness
Keep Fit Association, 1 Grove House, Foundry Lane, Horsham,
West Sussex RH13 5PL. Tel: 01403 266000
www.keepfit.org.uk

Angling
Angling Trust, Eastwood House, 6 Rainbow Street, Leominster,
Herefordshire HR6 8DQ. Tel: 0844 7700616.
www.anglingtrust.net

Archery
Archery GB, Lilleshall National Sports Centre, Nr Newport,
Shropshire TF10 9AT. Tel: (01952) 677888.
www.archerygb.org

Athletics
UK Athletics, Athletics House, Central Boulevard, Blythe Valley
Park, Solihull, West Midlands B90 8AJ. Tel: 0121 713 8400.
www.uka.org.uk

Badminton
Badminton England, National Badminton Centre, Milton Keynes
MK8 9LA. Tel: (01908) 268400.
www.badmintonengland.co.uk

Basketball
England Basketball, PO Box 3971, Sheffield S9 9AZ.
Tel: 0114 284 1060 www.englandbasketball.co.uk

Billiards (see snooker)

Boxing
British Boxing Board of Control, 14 North Road, Cardiff CF10
3DY. Tel: (029) 20 367000. www.bbbofc.com

Canoeing

British Canoe Union HQ (also the offices of Canoe England),
    18 Market Place, Bingham, Nottingham NG13 8AP.
    Tel: 0845 370 9500 or 0300 0119 500. www.bcu.org.uk/

Caving and rock climbing

British Caving Association, The Old Methodist Chapel, Great
    Hucklow, Buxton SK17 8RG. Tel: 01298 873810
    www.bcra.org.uk

Cricket

England and Wales Cricket Board, Lord's Cricket Ground,
    London NW8 8QZ. Tel: 020 7432 1200. www.ecb.co.uk

Cycling (including BMX and mountain biking)

British Cycling, National Cycling Centre, Stuart Street,
    Manchester M11 4DQ. Tel: 0161 274 2000.
    www.britishcycling.org.uk

Equestrianism

The British Horse Society, Abbey Park, Stareton, Kenilworth,
    Warks CV8 2XZ. Tel: 0844 848 1666. www.bhs.org.uk

Fencing

British Fencing Association, 1 Baron's Gate, 33–35 Rothschild
    Rd, London W4 5HT. Tel: (020) 8742 3032.
    www.britishfencing.com

Football (see American football, Aussie Rules, soccer, etc.)

Golf

English Golf Union Ltd, The National Golf Centre,
    Woodhall Spa, Lincs LN10 6PU. Tel: (01526) 354500.
    www.englishgolfunion.org or Professional Golfers'
    Association www.pga.info

123 The High Street
Thistown
Yorkshire QE2 6PE
Tel: 0123 456789

28 February 201X

Mr J Newbody
The National Coach
Newsport Headquarters

Dear Mr Anybody,

I am interested in playing newsport in a European country for the coming season and I wondered if you might be able to suggest someone I can contact or advise me on my best course of action.

I have three A levels, one of which is German which I also speak fluently, so my preferred countries are Austria, Germany and Switzerland, but I am happy to apply to other EEC countries as well.

I am 18 years old and for the past two years I have played in the Northern League for Thistown United. Last season I was voted their Most Valued Player.

It is my intention to gain experience whilst working abroad before applying to university to study for a sports science degree.

I would be very grateful for your assistance but if you are unable to help could you please send me the addresses of the newsport governing bodies in Austria, Germany and Switzerland.

Thank you for your assistance.

I look forward to hearing from you.

Yours sincerely,

John Jones

John Jones

Fig. 5. Sample letter to a national governing body.

Gymnastics
British Gymnastics, Ford Hall, Lilleshall Sports Centre, Newport,
   Shrops TF10 9NB. Tel: 0845 1297129.
   www.british-gymnastics.org

Handball
British Handball Association, Elwick Club, Church Road,
   Ashford, Kent TN23 1RD. Tel: 01233 878099
   www.Britishhandball.com

Hang gliding and paragliding
The British Hang Gliding and Paragliding Association Ltd.,
   8 Merus Court, Meridian Business Park, Leicester LE19 1RJ.
   Tel: 0116 289 4316. www.bhpa.co.uk

Hockey
England Hockey, Bisham Abbey National Sports Centre, Near
   Marlow, Buckinghamshire SL7 1RR. Tel: 01628 897500.
   www.englandhockey.co.uk

Horse riding (see equestrianism)

Ice hockey
Ice Hockey UK, 19 Heather Avenue, Rise Park, Romford, RM1
   4SL. Tel: 07917 194 264. www.icehockeyuk.co.uk

Judo
British Judo Association, Suite B, Loughborough Technical Park,
   Epinal Way, Loughborough LE11 3GE. Tel: (01509) 631670.
   www.britishjudo.org.uk

Karate
BKA, 149 Longsight, Harwood, Bolton BL2 3JE.
   Tel: 01484 843400. www.thebka.co.uk

Lacrosse
English Lacrosse, Belle Vue Centre, Pink Bank Lane, Longsight,
   Manchester M12 5GL. Tel: 0161 2273626.

www.englishlacrosse.co.uk

Modern pentathlon
MPAGB, Norwood House, University of Bath, Claverton Down, Bath BA2 7AY. Tel: (01225) 386808. www.mpagb.org.uk

Motor sports
The Royal Automobile Club Motor Sports Association Limited, Motor Sports House, Riverside Park, Colnbrook SL3 0HG. Tel: (01753) 765000. www.msauk.org

Mountain biking (see cycling)

Mountaineering
British Mountaineering Council, 177–179 Burton Road, Manchester M20 2BB. Tel: 0161 4456111. www.thebmc.co.uk

Netball
England Netball, Netball House, 9 Paynes Park, Hitchin, Herts, SG5 1EH. Tel: (01462) 442344. www.england-netball.co.uk

Orienteering
British Orienteering Federation, 8a Stancliffe House, Whitworth Road, Darley Dale, Matlock, Derbyshire DE4 2HJ. Tel: (01629) 734042. www.britishorienteering.org.uk

Parachuting
British Parachute Association, 5 Wharf Way, Glen Parva, Leicester LE2 9TF. Tel: (0116) 278 5271. www.bpa.org.uk

Rowing
British Rowing, 6 Lower Mall, Hammersmith, London W6 9DJ. Tel: 020 8237 6749 7100. www.britishrowing.org

Rugby League
Rugby Football League, Red Hall, Red Hall Lane, Leeds LS17 8NB. Tel: 0844 4777113. www.therfl.co.uk

Rugby Union

Rugby Football Union, Rugby House, Twickenham Stadium, 200 Whitton Road, Twickenham, Middlesex TW2 7BA. Tel: 0871 222 2120. www.rfu.com

Sailing

Royal Yachting Association, Ensign Way, Hamble, Southampton SO31 4YA. Tel: 023 8060 4100. www.rya.org.uk

Skiing and snowboarding

Snowsport England, Area Library Building, Halesowen, West Midlands B63 4AJ. Tel: (0121) 501 2314. www.snowsportengland.org.uk

Snooker and billiards

English Association of Snooker and Billiards, Cedar House, Cedar Lane, Frimley, Surrey GU16 7HY. Tel: 0808 1294040. www.englishsnooker.com

Soccer

The Football Association, Wembley Stadium, PO Box 1966, London SW1P 9EQ. Tel: no phone number given. www.thefa.com

Squash (and racquetball)

National Squash Centre, Sportcity, Manchester M11 3FF. Tel: 0161 231 4499. www.englandsquashandracketball.com

Surfing

British Surfing Association., Fistral Beach, Newquay, Cornwall TR7 1HY. Tel: (01637) 876474. www.britsurf.co.uk

Swimming (life saving listed under National Bodies – below)

ASA HQ, SportPark, 3 Oakwood Drive, Loughborough, Leicestershire LE11 3QF. Tel: 01509 618 700. www.swimming.org

Table tennis
English Table Tennis Association, 3rd Floor, Queensbury House,
Havelock Road, Hastings, East Sussex TN34 1HF.
Tel: (01424) 722525 www.etta.tv

Ten pin bowling
British Ten Pin Bowling Association, 114 Balfour Road, Ilford,
Essex IG1 4JD. Tel: (020) 8478 1745. www.btba.org.uk

Tennis
The Lawn Tennis Association, 100 Priory Lane, Roehampton,
London SW15 5JQ Tel: 020 8487 7000. www.lta.org.uk

Trampolining (see gymnastics)

Volleyball
English Volleyball Association, SportPark, 3 Oakwood Drive,
Loughborough LE11 3QF. Tel: 01509 227722.
www.volleyballengland.org

Waterskiing and wakeboarding
British Water Ski and Wakeboard, The Forum, Hanworth Lane,
Chertsey, Surrey KT16 9JX. Tel: 01932 560007.
www.britishwaterski.org.uk

Weightlifting
BWLA, 119 Cavendish Hall, Leeds Metropolitan University,
Headingley Campus, Leeds, West Yorkshire LS6 3QS.
Tel: 0776 6918239. www.bwla.co.uk

Windsurfing (see sailing)

NATIONAL ORGANISING BODIES
Association of Chartered Physiotherapists in Sports Medicine.
Contact by email only. www.acpsm.org

British Red Cross, UK Office, 44 Moorfields, London
EC2Y 9AL. Tel: 0844 871 1111. www.redcross.org.uk

British Universities and Colleges Sport (BUCS) 20–24 Kings
Bench Street, London SE1 0QX. Tel: 020 7633 5080.
www.bucs.org.uk

BUSA (British Universities Sports Association) has now changed
to (BUCS) (see above).

The Central Council of Physical Recreation (CCPR), Burwood
House, 14–16 Caxton Street, London SW1H 0QT.
Tel: 020 7976 3900. www.ccpr.org.uk

The Chartered Society of Physiotherapy, CSP, 14 Bedford Row,
London WC1R 4ED. Tel: (020) 7306 6666. www.csp.org.uk

City and Guilds, 1 Giltspur Street, London EC1A 9DD.
Tel: 0844 543 0000. www.city-and-guilds.co.uk

The Institute for Outdoor Learning, Warwick Mill Business
Centre, Warwick Bridge, Carlisle, Cumbria CA4 8RR.
Tel: 01228 564580. www.outdoor-learning.org

Learn Direct, PO Box 900, Leicester LE1 6XJ. Tel: 0800 101 902.
www.learndirect.co.uk

Professional Footballers' Association. Tel: 0161 236 0575.
www.gimmefootball.com

Royal Life Saving Society, Lifesavers, River House, High Street,
Broom, Warwickshire B50 4HN. Tel: (01789) 773994.
www.lifesavers.org.uk

Sports Coach UK, 114 Cardigan Road, Headingley, Leeds
LS6 3BJ. Tel: (0113) 274 4802. www.sportscoachuk.org

St. John Ambulance Brigade, 27 St. John's Lane, London
EC1M 4BU. Tel: 08700 104950. www.sja.org.uk

You might need to write a letter, as shown in Figure 6, for one of many reasons. This one is shown as an example of how to acquire more qualifications.

CONTACTING A BRITISH UNIVERSITY WHICH OFFERS SPORTS SCHOLARSHIPS

An outline of what is on offer is given in more detail in Chapter 2. Below are the addresses of colleges and universities that have recently offered sports scholarships and bursaries.

---

123 The High Street
Thistown
Yorkshire QE2 6PE
Tel: 0123 456789

28 February 201X

The British Red Cross
National Headquarters

Dear Sir,

I am interested in taking a course that will lead to becoming qualified in first aid. Unfortunately I haven't been able to obtain this information from either my local library or through local newspapers.

Could you please provide me with the contact address of the local organiser of these courses and, if possible, let me know the dates they run, and the cost of enrolment.

Thank you for your assistance.

I look forward to hearing from you.

Yours sincerely,

John Jones

John Jones

Fig. 6. Sample letter to a national organising body.

If you have problems accessing the information you need, contact the British Universities and Colleges Sport (BUCS) 20–24 Kings Bench Street, London SE1 0QX. Tel: 020 7633 5080. www.bucs.org.uk for advice.

The University of Aberdeen, King's College, Aberdeen
　　AB24 3FX. Tel: 01224 272000. www.abdn.ac.uk
Aberystwyth University, Old College, King Street, Aberystwyth,
　　SY23 2AX. Tel: 01970 623111. www.aber.ac.uk
Bangor University, Bangor, Gwynedd LL57 2DG.
　　Tel: 01248 351151. www.bangor.ac.uk
University of Bath, Sports Development & Recreation, Bath
　　BA2 7AY. Tel: 01225 386656. www.bath.ac.uk
University of Birmingham Sport, Munrow Sports Centre,
　　Edgbaston B15 2TT. Tel: 0121 4144117.
　　www.sport.bham.ac.uk
University of Bristol, Senate House, Tyndall Avenue, Bristol
　　BS8 1TH. Tel: 0117 928 9000. www.bris.ac.uk
Brunel University, Kingston Lane, Uxbridge, Middlesex
　　UB8 3PH. Tel: 01895 274000. www.brunel.ac.uk
University of Cambridge, The Old Schools, Trinity Lane,
　　Cambridge CB2 1TN. Check website for individual college's
　　telephone numbers. www.cam.ac.uk
Cardiff University, Cardiff, Wales CF10 3XQ. Tel: 029 208 74000.
　　www.cardiff.ac.uk
Coventry University, Priory Street, Coventry CV1 5FB.
　　Tel: 024 7688 7688. www.coventry.ac.uk
De Montfort University, The Gateway, Leicester LE1 9BH.
　　Tel: 0116 255 1551. www.dmu.ac.uk
Durham University, University Office, Old Elvet, Durham
　　DH1 3HP. Tel: 0191 3346141. www.dur.ac.uk
Edinburgh University, Old College, South Bridge Edinburgh
　　EH8 9YL. Tel: 0131 650 1000. www.ed.ac.uk

University of Exeter, Streatham Campus, Northcote House,
Exeter EX4 4QJ. Tel: 01392 661000. www.sport.exeter.ac.uk
Glasgow University, Glasgow, Scotland G12 8QQ.
Tel. 0141 330 2000. www.gla.ac.uk
Heriot-Watt University, Edinburgh Campus, Scotland EH14 4AS.
Tel: 0131 449 5111. www.hw.ac.uk
Leeds Metropolitan University, Civic Quarter, Leeds LS1 3HE.
Tel: 0113 812 3113. www.leedsmet.ac.uk
Loughborough University, Leicestershire LE11 3TU.
Tel: 01509 263171. www.lboro.ac.uk
University of Manchester, Moseley Road, Fallowfield, Manchester
M14 6HE. Tel: 0161 306 9988. www.sport.manchester.ac.uk
Newcastle University, NE1 7RU. Tel: 0191 222 6000.
www.ncl.ac.uk
University of Northumbria, Ellison Place, Newcastle upon Tyne,
NE1 8ST. Tel: 0191 232 6002. www.northumbria.ac.uk
University of Oxford Sport, Jackdaw Lane, Iffley Road, Oxford
OX4 1EQ. Tel: 01865 240476. www.sport.ox.ac.uk
Queen's University, University Road, Belfast, Northern Ireland
BT7 1NN. Tel: 028 90245133. www.qub.ac.uk
University of Reading, Whiteknights, PO Box 217, Reading
RG6 6AH. Tel: 0118 987 5123. www.reading.ac.uk
St. Andrews University, College Gate, St Andrews, Fife
KY16 9AJ. Tel: 01334 476161. www.st-andrews.ac.uk
Stirling University, Stirling, Scotland FK9 4LA.
Tel: 01786 473171. www.external.stir.ac.uk
University of Strathclyde, 76 Southbrae Drive, Glasgow G13 1PP.
Tel: 0141 9503000. www.strath.ac.uk
University of Sunderland, Edinburgh Building, Chester Road,
Sunderland SR1 3SD. Tel: 0191 515 2000.
www.sunderland.ac.uk
University of Surrey, Guildford, Surrey GU2 7XH.
Tel: 01483 300800. www.portal.surrey.ac.uk

Swansea University, Singleton Park, Swansea, Wales SA2 8PP.
   Tel: 01792 205678. www.swansea.ac.uk
Teesside University, Middlesbrough, Tees Valley TS1 3BA.
   Tel: 01642 218121. www.tees.ac.uk
University of Ulster, York Street, Belfast, Co. Antrim BT15 1ED.
   Tel: 028 70123456. www.ulster.ac.uk
University of Wales, King Edward VII Avenue, Cardiff
   CF10 3NS. Tel: 029 2037 6999. www.wales.ac.uk
University of Wales, Caerleon Campus, Lodge Road, Caerleon
   NP18 3QT. Tel: 01633 432432. www.newport.ac.uk
University of Worcester, Henwick Grove, Worcester WR2 6AJ.
   Tel: 01905 855 000. www.worcester.ac.uk

CONTACTING AN OVERSEAS UNIVERSITY OFFERING SPORTS SCHOLARSHIPS

The number of universities and colleges around the world offering sports scholarships is so numerous that to include details of them all would be beyond the scope of this book.

However, information on opportunities in the USA is easily accessed through the numerous internet search engines, or alternatively by reading *Sports Scholarships and College Programs in the USA*: editor Ron Walker, by Peterson's Guides. This can be borrowed from most main libraries or purchased from the UK distributor Vacation Work Publications.

Scholarships in other parts of the world are now becoming more abundant and can also be easily accessed through the internet. Either type the name of the university or country that you are interested in into a search engine (MSN, Google, Lycos, etc.) or table a general request such as 'Sports Scholarships Abroad' and it will come up with an extensive list, many of them commercial companies that have the required details, so check out the free sites first.

7

Ensuring You Have the Necessary Qualifications

There are no qualifications required for a professional playing career in any sport, just outstanding ability. Unfortunately, though, successful careers can be cut short, at any time, by injury. Bear in mind also that any sports career that extends beyond seven years is considered to be a long one. It would be foolish therefore to ignore gaining qualifications, or experience, that would assist in developing a new career once the professional sporting one is over. Many soccer clubs acknowledge this and insist that their apprentice professionals study for educational qualifications.

OBTAINING GENERAL QUALIFICATIONS

It is advisable to study for recognised qualifications awarded by reputable bodies. Some of these are detailed below. If you want to pursue a career in coaching or instructing it would be sensible to hold a certificate from your national body. Details of these follow under 'Acquiring National Coaching Awards'.

To gain employment in certain careers you need to study for a certificate or diploma organised by a recognised body within that profession. Details are given below under 'Gaining Professional Qualifications'.

A 'vocational' qualification concentrates on job-related skills and knowledge, compared to an 'academic' qualification which reflects a depth of study in a much narrower subject area.

A very brief guide to some of the qualifications available is given below. For more expansive information log on to Education & Learning at www.direct.gov.uk

GCSE

Normally taken when you are at school, so the majority of young people reading this book should already have experience of these and hopefully have gained some passes. However, if you feel that you should have done better, for whatever reason, all is not lost. Most towns have at least one facility where you can resit or even take further examinations. Look them up in *Yellow Pages* under Schools and Colleges.

You may think it is a little unjust, but details of these qualifications will be needed for the rest of your working life. Even when applying for a job aged 50 the employer will ask you what school examination passes you achieved. So it is very important that you do as well as you can in these.

Some of you will have succeeded at GCSE and obtained good grades at 'A' level too. This is an added bonus as more opportunities will be available to you.

OCR Nationals

OCR Nationals are normally studied at school, the target students being teenagers (14–19), but the qualifications are also suitable for adult learners, much like the GNVQ.

They are vocationally related qualifications which were officially launched in September 2004. The qualifications are designed to meet the needs of those seeking work-related qualifications in place of the traditional, theory intensive, academic ones.

OCR Nationals are available at Levels 1, 2 and 3, and were intended to be an alternative to GNVQs, which have now been withdrawn.

As well as sport-based qualifications, others are also available in business, design, health and social care, information technology, leisure travel & tourism, media, public services, and science.

Qualifications after you have left school

Once you have left school – with or without GCSEs – there is a whole load of other qualifications that you could obtain, many of them through sports-related courses.

The range and number of these courses can be quite confusing so, in an attempt to simplify them, the following general rules can be applied under the assumption that we are confining ourselves to sports-related study.

◆ City and Guilds courses offer, amongst other things, qualifications to work in sports centres.

◆ Business and Technician Education Council (BTEC) courses are aimed at people who want the option of going into higher education sports studies.

◆ National Vocation Qualification (NVQ) courses offer a practical, work-based type of study and are popular with those who are interested in working in tourism. In Scotland they are called SVQ.

The above is a very simplified explanation of these courses and there is a significant amount of overlap and integration between them. You may take a qualification with one examining body, but have to transfer to a different one to achieve the final diploma that you require. For example, the BTEC First Diploma in Sports Studies qualifies you to go on to the BTEC National Diploma in Sports Studies.

All this can be very confusing and, in order to make it clearer, further details of these awards are given below.

To further complicate things, at the end of 2010, vocational qualifications such as BTECs, City and Guilds and OCR Nationals are being updated and will be available as new qualifications on the Qualifications and Credit Framework (QCF).

City and Guilds

This is a vocationally based qualification with a small amount of academic content that can be studied at four different levels – Parts 1, 2, 3 and 4, with the last being the most academically demanding and hardest to pass. By comparison Part 1 is very practical and easier to pass. You should not need any other qualifications to enrol on these courses although, especially if the demand is high, this may be at the discretion of your local college.

These awards are long established and recognised by all British-owned companies abroad. Many foreign companies also recognise them, but this will differ from country to country.

If you would like more information contact your local school, college, or the City and Guilds Institute (see Chapter 6). Their most popular course is Recreation and Leisure Studies so expect competition if you are applying for it. For more information log on to www.cityandguilds.com

BTEC

BTEC, which stands for the Business and Technician Education Council, concerns itself with numerous vocational qualifications including Leisure, Recreation and Management. These qualifications are recognised, in a similar fashion to City and Guilds, throughout Britain and by British owned companies abroad – although in Scotland they have their own version under SCQF (Scottish Credit and Qualifications Framework).

BTEC has five levels of qualification ranging from Level One – the First Diploma or Certificate, up to Level Five – the Continuing Education Certificate (CEC). The BTEC First Diploma is equivalent to City and Guilds Part Two. The BTEC Level Three is equivalent to City and Guilds Part Four and also considered equivalent to the first year of a degree course.

No educational qualifications are normally required to enrol for a First Diploma level course. Most colleges accept candidates on the strength of their interview and references from their old school.

Further information can be obtained by contacting your local school, college, or the BTEC or SCQF bodies or by reading some of the relevant books in Chapter 10. *A Guide to Jobs and Qualifications in Sport and Recreation* by John Potter/ILAM is particularly recommended.

NVQ

The National Vocational Qualification, and the SVQ in Scotland, were originally intended to replace the BTEC and the City and Guilds, and for a while there was a confusing overlap between them all. This appears to have been rectified to some extent by the examining boards specialising in different fields, so if your career choice was to work in tourism you would initially take an NVQ course.

The NVQ awards tend to be more practical 'hands on' courses.

More advanced awards

There are other, higher-level qualifications offered in addition to those covered above, but you need to have some of the previously detailed qualifications before you can apply for them. You can get the information on these more advanced courses from your school, college or course tutor, or by accessing www.direct.gov.uk/en/EducationAndLearning

GAINING PROFESSIONAL QUALIFICATIONS

Once you have secured a job, promotion within it is often gained due to experience or attaining higher or professional qualifications. You could progress by gaining a Higher National Diploma, a Higher National Certificate, the Certificate of Management Studies (CMS), the ILAM Certificate of Leisure Operations, the Continuing Education Certificate (CEC), the ILAM Certificate of Leisure Management, the National Examination Board for Supervisory Management (NEBSM), university degree, postgraduate diploma, master's degree, doctorate, etc. The list continues to expand at a rapid pace every year.

Most employers have their own personnel department which will advise you on your own career development. If you need further advice read *A Guide to Jobs and Qualifications in Sport and Recreation* by John Potter/ILAM or other relevant books in the further reading section. You could also contact your local school, college, or career advisors.

ACQUIRING NATIONAL COACHING AWARDS

Many beginners-level awards are quite easy to achieve, aren't too time-consuming and are also quite inexpensive.

For example the Coaching Assistant Award in Athletics lasts just two days and after this you are qualified to coach youngsters under the supervision of a club coach. There is no exam and the price for this in 2010 was £130 for affiliated club members and that includes a manual for the course. If you wanted to be able to coach without the supervision then this takes a little longer and is obviously more demanding. More details are available on coaching.uka.org.uk.

If you are interested in applying for a different coaching award, you should refer to the list of organisers in Chapter 6.

ADDING OTHER LESS FORMAL QUALIFICATIONS

Any qualification, no matter how insignificant you think it is, should be used to promote yourself to prospective employers. Many employers are just as impressed by applicants who hold other types of qualifications, as they reflect personal qualities not always found in academic or vocational awards.

Even just a swimming certificate or a typing course that you have passed could be useful. For example, if two people are applying for the same job, and both have the same academic qualifications to offer, then these little extras might just tip the scales to your advantage.

Don't forget if you are travelling, and intend to be changing jobs, carry these documents with you.

Some of the more useful ones, that should be noted on your application form or at an interview, are listed below. This is by no means a complete list. Gaining these simple qualifications not only opens up a multitude of job opportunities, but will also enhance your own lifestyle.

Driving licence

Many employers expect their employees to hold a current driving licence and, for insurance purposes, they often prefer the holder to be over 21 years old (in some cases over 25) and to have no convictions, driving or otherwise.

First aid

The basic first aid certificate is quite easy to pass and is highly valued by employers. They feel more at ease knowing that their staff are able to deal with accidents and emergencies.

Employment agencies often stipulate that candidates must possess first aid qualifications whilst others, particularly in the tourist industry, are keen to advertise in their glossy brochures that all of their staff possess first aid certificates.

If you would like to take one of these awards, or would simply like more information, look up the address and telephone number of your local Red Cross or St John Ambulance organisations on the internet or in the telephone directory. If you can't locate them by these methods, details of their head offices are in Chapter 6.

Life saving

Awards in life saving are absolutely essential if you are going to be involved with instructing or assisting with any watersports.

It is also looked on favourably by most other sports-oriented employers as it offers greater flexibility in the range of work that you are able to do for them. Even if you are only applying to hand out deckchairs on a beach, holding one of these awards will tip the scales in your favour during the interview.

If you would like to take this award then contact your local swimming baths for details. Their telephone number will be in your local directory. Alternatively, you can contact the head office of the Royal Life Saving Society, details of which are in Chapter 6.

Languages

If you intend to work abroad, speaking the local language has a most distinct advantage. Most positions of responsibility are advertised with this as a prerequisite for applying. Not all employers, however, ask for formal qualifications. They might ask merely for an ability to speak the language, in which case you can expect to be tested during the interview.

Even if you do not speak the language before applying all is not lost. Put an application in, stating that you have a basic command of the language. Then start cramming up by using a phrase book and/or a computer or CD/DVD language course. If you are given an interview, stress that you are willing to enrol at your local college on a language course to improve. This will impress the interviewer that you are a conscientious prospective employee, and they will also realise that once you are living in the country your language skills will improve enormously in a relatively short time.

Other less formal qualifications

Almost any qualification or hobby is worth putting down on the application form or in your CV. Obviously these will be more useful if they relate directly to work that you are going to do. For example, you might not be a qualified mechanic, but if you have had a lifelong hobby of rebuilding old cars then your employer would probably consider this advantageous in someone who is applying for a driving job with their company and who may be able to fix minor faults immediately.

However, even if you think your qualification might not be relevant, still put it down as this just might help you to get the job. You never know, the company which is interviewing you for a job as a lifeguard in their swimming pool might also be looking for someone who has computer skills to help cope with the administrative aspects of the job.

LOOKING AFTER REFERENCES AND TESTIMONIALS

References are asked for by all employers and are provided by referees nominated by you. They are confidential and you rarely see them. Testimonials are 'open' references that you can get from someone in authority – teacher, youth worker, sports coach, etc. – and are either included with your application, or are shown during the interview. If you have one of these in your possession it is vital that it is kept in good condition for future use. Remember, this is what impresses an employer and can often be the difference between being called for interview or having your application thrown in the bin.

SUMMARY

Qualifications
◆ Make sure your qualifications are suitable for the employment that you seek.

◆ Rectify any deficiencies by going on courses.

◆ Acquire the easier, less formal, qualifications like first aid. It just might tip the scales in your favour.

References and testimonials
◆ References and testimonials are very important. Get good ones and keep them safe and clean.

Language
◆ If you intend working abroad, start to learn the language and let prospective employers know this.

8

Securing the Job

MAKING THE INITIAL CONTACT

Once you have found a job or position that is of interest to you, your next task is to contact the person who advertised it. If you are applying to a big company it will probably have its own application form and you simply write a brief letter to the person named, asking for one. Examples of this type of letter and a company application form are given later in this chapter.

However, if you are writing to an employer or a smaller company which doesn't produce its own application form it would be advisable to use the following procedure.

Write to them personally and under no circumstances send them a standard, obviously duplicated, letter. Most employers would take this as a sign that you are not particularly interested in their job, but simply after any work that comes along, and that if you have put in so many applications that you needed to duplicate them you might already have employment by the time they reply.

Making the right impression

Figure 7 is an example of a letter to a small company, in this case based in France. If you are fluent in French, write this letter in French to prove you have linguistic skills. You should also send them your curriculum vitae (CV), the names of referees and any testimonials that you have, and a recent photograph, even if they are not asked for. This shows you are organised and have nothing to hide. It also helps to jump the queue on other applicants who are later asked to supply these.

11 Oxford Street
Uptown
Surrey UP2 4YU
Tel: 0198 765432

28 February 201X

Monsieur Didier St Jean
Manager, Hotel Belle Vue
Valmorel, France.

Monsicur,

I am interested in the position of chalet maid that you advertised in *Skiing World*.

As can see from the enclosed curriculum vitae, I am very experienced in domestic work for ski companies as this will be my fourth season. Three of these seasons were in Italy, however, so my command of the French language is basic. I can manage to make myself understood at the supermarket and around town. However before taking up any employment I will be enrolling on a French course to improve this. I anticipate that by the end of this winter I will be relatively fluent. After three seasons in Italy, I speak Italian quite fluently.

I am keen to work in France as I enjoy the French culture and one of my passions is skiing which I hope to do in my spare time.

I would be grateful if you would consider me for interview or advise me on the next stage of the application.

I look forward to hearing from you.

Yours faithfully,

Michelle Morrison

Michelle Morrison

Fig. 7. Sample letter to an individual or small company.

The initial contact is all about making the right impression, so
here is some advice.

DO	DON'T
Write in the appropriate language when applying abroad, if you can.	Presume that people from other countries speak English. This is often interpreted as arrogance.
Produce your letter on a computer or word processor if possible.	Write it on paper that has been ripped out of a notepad or similar.
If you handwrite it make sure it is neat, clean and easily understood.	Write it in any colour other than black or blue. Some people will be greatly offended if it is written in red or green.
Write it formally. Address the recipient Dear Sir, Dear Madam, Dear Mr... or Dear Mrs...	Even if the advert includes their christian name, address them as Tony or Dear Liz. This shows a lack of respect and the employer may presume that you could be disrespectful at work.
If you've addressed the recipient as Dear Mr Smith you finish the letter with 'Yours sincerely'. If you started with Dear Sir you finish the letter with 'Yours faithfully'.	Finish the letter with just 'Yours' or 'See you soon' or similar.
Print your name under the signature.	Just sign the letter. Your signature may look perfectly legible to you, but it can be unreadable to some one else. The recipient might therefore not know who to address the reply to, and consequently not bother.
Include all the information the application form asks for.	Presume there are some things that your prospective employer doesn't need to know. It may hinder your chances or make it appear that you are trying to hide something.

COMPOSING YOUR CV

A CV is simply a record of you: your achievements, leisure activities and employment.

You will see from the example later in this chapter that it is normally written in reverse order, starting with your most recent achievements and normally finishing at the date you started secondary education. If you have any difficulty composing your CV there are numerous books in the library dealing with this subject, or you can get advice from your local school, college, careers company, or job seekers' club. A job seekers' club is usually located at your local Jobcentre.

Getting the CV typed

If you don't own a computer, word processor or typewriter contact your local job seekers' club, school or college as they will probably be able to help you. They might also be able to supply you with numerous printouts or photocopies for reference. If this fails look in your local free paper for somebody advertising 'professional CVs produced' – or something similar. There are normally several of these. It is better to pay a few pounds to them, and create the right impression, than to lose the job. They will also make you multiple copies of your CV so that you have spares to use for other applications.

Compiling your CV

Take your time when compiling your CV. Prepare it thoroughly. Your success depends on it. Other applicants for the job may have inferior qualifications to you, but appear to be better because of a superior CV.

Don't tell lies in your CV, but experiment with ways of making a better impression. For example, look at the work experience of Jane in the sample CV in this chapter. Her first job was stacking shelves in a supermarket when they became low on stock. She could have called herself a shelf stacker, but stock control assistant sounds much better.

Other points to observe are as follows:

◆ Don't make your CV too long. Two or three sides of A4 paper are sufficient. If yours runs to more than this you must edit it. A prospective employer doesn't want to wade through page after page of waffle.

◆ Produce it on good quality paper. It gives the recipient the impression that you have made a special effort and that their job is important to you.

◆ Don't send a photocopy of your CV, unless it is a very, very good one. The quality of the paper is often poor. The print may also be grey rather than dark. The employer will get the impression that you have sent out scores of applications and their job is nothing special.

◆ Avoid technical jargon, the employer may not know what you mean.

◆ Avoid slang. He may understand what you mean – but will not be impressed.

Altering your CV

The example in Figure 8 is not the only way to construct a CV. You can alter the headings to suit your qualifications and experience. However, most CVs generally follow this pattern.

If you do change this structure try several different formats and get a relative or friend to look it over. It must look neat, professional and contain all the vital information. It must also present you in the most favourable light possible.

Name:	Jane Jobseeker,
Address:	123 High Stret, Workborough, Wessex WE2 4UP
Tel:	01234 567890
Date of birth:	29 February 1988
Nationality:	British
Education:	2004–2006. Workborough Sixth Form College, Green Lane, Workborough.
	A Levels: English Language (B), Mathematics (C), French (C)
	1999–2004 Wessex School, Early Road, Workborough.
	GCSEs: English Language (A), Mathematics (B), French (B), German (C), Science (C), Geography (C), History (C).
Work experience:	Cutprice Supermarket, Sept 2004 to present date. Friday evenings and weekends. Started as stock control assistant in 2004 and recently promoted to cashier
Interests:	Member of St John Ambulance Brigade. Competition standard at both basketball and horse riding.
Other information:	I hold current St John First Aid Certificate.
	I hold provisional driving licence – taking test in three weeks' time.
	I am currently studying for the National Basketball Coaches Award.

Fig. 8. Sample CV.

FILLING IN THE APPLICATION FORM

Always complete the form in black or blue ink, unless it
specifically states on the form that it should be typewritten.
Always write in capital letters, again unless specified differently.
Read the application form thoroughly before starting to fill it in.
It is often better to write a draft copy first on scrap paper,
correcting any mistakes and making any alterations on that
rather than the form itself. An application form full of alterations
and mistakes immediately gives the impression that your work is
slapdash and you will almost undoubtedly lose the job.

In your excitement to apply for your dream job you may be
tempted to mail the application as soon as possible. This often
leads to things being missed off that you later realise would have
been advantageous to include. Rushing also often leads to untidy
writing and a badly constructed application. All of this can be
easily avoided.

- First, deliberately take your time. One extra day delay will
  probably make no difference at all, but a shoddy application will.

- Secondly, before you write anything on the form, write it on
  another sheet of paper to see if it looks right. If in doubt, get
  someone else's opinion.

- Think of everything. Too much is better than too little. If it
  helps, refer back to Chapter 1.

- Double check. Make sure you've included all of your skills,
  qualifications and experience on the rough sheet before
  transferring it to the application form.

Don't forget that the employer will probably get many more
applications than there are jobs available so before they draw up

a shortlist they have to reduce this number. Don't give them any excuse to eliminate yours.

A specimen application for P.G.L. Ltd., is shown in Figure 9 and will give you an idea of what to expect.

SUPPLYING REFERENCES

This was covered in Chapters 1 and 7. Refer to those sections again if you need to.

However, please remember that the terms 'reference' and 'testimonial' often get confused so check exactly what your interviewer requires.

OBTAINING AN INTERVIEW

It is not unusual for it to take quite some time before you receive a reply to your job application. Don't worry about it. Remember that employers are very busy people and will have received many applications. If they are conscientious they will read every application before compiling a shortlist for interview. What may seem like weeks of waiting to you is probably much less. It always seems longer when you are anxious, but don't let this waiting time be wasted time.

Presume that you have been unsuccessful with this application and continue to look for other jobs. This not only makes the days go faster, but also prepares you for the worst. Imagine, though, the delight if you are wrong and a letter later arrives offering an interview!

 **APPLICATION FORM**

First read through the details and then complete all sections as fully as possible even if you have attached other information such as a CV. If you require assistance in completing this form, for example if you have a disability, please contact the PGL Recruitment Team who will be happy to help you. This will in no way be detrimental to your application.

➤ PERSONAL DETAILS

SURNAME

FORENAMES (underline used name)

Are you 18 or over? Yes ☐ No ☐

DATE OF BIRTH (Optional, unless you are under 18 at the time of applying)

TITLE: MR/MISS/MRS/MS/OTHER:

➤ ADDRESSES
(at which you can be contacted between now and your given start date)

HOME BETWEEN THE DATES OF

ADDRESS

DAYTIME TEL (including STD Code)

EVENING TEL

MOBILE

EMAIL
If you would like to receive PGL's Recruitment E-news please tick ☐

TEMPORARY BETWEEN THE DATES OF

ADDRESS

DAYTIME TEL (including STD Code)

EVENING TEL

MOBILE

EMAIL

➤ LEGAL ELIGIBILITY

Under the Asylum and Immigration Act 1996, it is unlawful for PGL Travel Ltd to employ anyone who does not have permission to work in the UK or the country they are applying for. All successful staff will be required to produce proof of identification on arrival at centre, e.g. passport, work permit or other legal documentation.

NATIONALITY

DO YOU HOLD A VALID EU PASSPORT? Yes ☐ No ☐

Passport Number: Expiry Date:

DO YOU HOLD A CURRENT WORK PERMIT/VISA?

Yes ☐ (please send a photocopy with your application) No ☐

Are you in the process of applying for one? Yes ☐ No ☐

PGL is unable to apply for a work visa/permit on your behalf.

➤ AVAILABILITY

Dates between which you are available for work (please give precise dates). If you can give the widest choice of dates it will increase our ability to place you.

FROM TO
Preference will be given to applicants able to start work between Jan-May.

Notice period required for current job, if applicable:

POSITIONS PREFERRED (For list of positions see PGL Recruitment brochure or www.pgl.co.uk/recruitment). If you are unsure which roles suit you best, please leave blank and a Recruitment Officer will call you for a chat.

1ST CHOICE

2ND CHOICE

3RD CHOICE

PREFERRED LOCATION OR CENTRES
Leave blank if you do not have a preference

1ST CHOICE

2ND CHOICE

3RD CHOICE

GENERAL

Are you applying with a friend? Yes ☐ No ☐

Friend's name

Will you accept the job without them? Yes ☐ No ☐

Have you worked for PGL previously? Yes ☐ No ☐

If Yes, what year?

Have you applied to work for PGL before? Yes ☐ No ☐

If Yes, what year?

➤ CONTACTING YOU
What is the best time of day to call you if we wish to discuss your application?

Anytime ☐ 8am - 1pm ☐ 1pm - 5pm ☐ After 5pm ☐

Although some formal documents must be sent to you by post, please tick your preferred method of receiving communication from us:

By post ☐ By email ☐

Fig. 9. Sample application form.

➤ ACADEMIC & VOCATIONAL QUALIFICATIONS

PLEASE LIST ALL YOUR ACADEMIC AND VOCATIONAL
QUALIFICATIONS E.G. GCSE'S. COLLEGE COURSES ETC.

(Use additional sheet if required)

➤ EMPLOYMENT

PLEASE LIST YOUR EMPLOYMENT HISTORY UP TO A
MAXIMUM OF THE PAST 7 YEARS, INCLUDING VACATION
AND VOLUNTARY WORK. EXPLAIN ANY GAPS.

CURRENT EMPLOYMENT

COMPANY

DATES   from   to

JOB TITLE / MAIN DUTIES

REASON FOR LEAVING

COMPANY

DATES   from   to

JOB TITLE

REASON FOR LEAVING

COMPANY

DATES   from   to

JOB TITLE

REASON FOR LEAVING

COMPANY

DATES   from   to

JOB TITLE

REASON FOR LEAVING
(Use additional sheet if required)

➤ DO YOU HOLD A FIRST AID CERTIFICATE?

Yes ❑ No ❑   (If yes please enclose a photocopy)

DATE PASSED:

TYPE OF CERIFICATE, I.E. FAAW:

➤ DO YOU HAVE A DRIVING LICENCE?

If Yes, please enclose a photocopy.

Yes ❑   No ❑   DATE PASSED:

MANUAL ❑   AUTOMATIC ❑

DOES THE LICENCE HAVE ANY ENDORSEMENTS?

                                   Yes ❑   No ❑
If Yes, please give **full details** on a separate sheet

DETAIL YOUR BREADTH OF DRIVING EXPERIENCE

DO YOU HAVE EXPERIENCE OF:

DRIVING MINIBUSES OR VANS   Yes ❑   No ❑

TOWING TRAILERS   Yes ❑   No ❑

DRIVING OVERSEAS   Yes ❑   No ❑

➤ LANGUAGES

	FLUENT	CONVERSATIONAL	BASIC
ENGLISH	❑	❑	❑
FRENCH	❑	❑	❑
SPANISH	❑	❑	❑
GERMAN	❑	❑	❑
ITALIAN	❑	❑	❑

HOW DID YOU ACQUIRE THIS LEVEL?

➤ PASTORAL EXPERIENCE

Please give details of your experience working /
volunteering with young people aged 7-17, your interests
and any positions of responsibility you have held:

(Use additional sheet if required)

Fig. 9. cont.

➤ **EXPERIENCE AND QUALIFICATIONS**

Please indicate your degree of competence by ticking the relevant column. Circle any of the listed qualifications that you hold and add any which are not listed. **Please send** photocopies of your qualifications with this application.

	BASIC	COMPETENT	QUALIFIED
■ DINGHY SAILING	☐	☐	☐

RYA Level Seamanship/4/5, AI, I, SI, other:

■ WINDSURFING	☐	☐	☐

RYA Level 2/3/4, Instructor Level A1/1/2/3, other:

Are you a member of the Royal Yachting Assoc.? Yes ☐ No ☐
Membership No.:

■ KAYAKING	☐	☐	☐

BCU 3 Star, 4 Star, Trainee Level 2 Coach, Level 2 Coach, Trainee Level 3 Coach, Level 3 Coach, other:

■ OPEN CANOEING (CANADIAN)	☐	☐	☐

BCU 3 Star, 4 Star, Trainee Level 2 Coach, Level 2 Coach, Trainee Level 3 Coach, Level 3 Coach, other:

■ SURF CANOEING	☐	☐	☐

BCU 3 Star, 4 Star, Trainee Level 2 Coach, Level 2 Coach, Trainee Level 3 Coach, Level 3 Coach, other:

Are you a member of the British Canoe Union? Yes ☐ No ☐
Membership No.:

■ SURFING	☐	☐	☐

BSA Level 1/2, other:

■ WHITE WATER RAFTING	☐	☐	☐

SRA Level 1/2/3, other:

■ RESCUE BOAT DRIVING	☐	☐	☐

RYA Powerboat Level 2, RYA Safety Boat Award, other:

■ LIFE SAVING	☐	☐	☐

RLSS Pool Lifeguard, RLSS Beach Lifeguard, other:

■ HILL WALKING/CLIMBING	☐	☐	☐

MLTB Summer Trained/Assessed, SPA Trained / Assessed other:

■ MOUNTAIN BIKING	☐	☐	☐

OTC, Other:

■ PONY TREKKING/HORSE RIDING	☐	☐

BHS Trek Leader, Prelim.Teacher, AI, WRTA Trek Header, Trek Escort, other:

■ SKIING	☐	☐	☐
■ SNOWBOARDING	☐	☐	☐

➤ **HOSPITALITY & EXPERIENCE**

Please give details of your catering, hospitality, administration, customer service or bar work experience.

[Use additional sheet if required]

➤ **PRACTICAL EXPERIENCE**

Please give details of your gardening, plumbing, DIY, electrical, carpentry, fibreglassing, maintenance or building experience.

[Use additional sheet if required]

Fig. 9. cont.

➤ YOUR SUITABILITY

As positions at PGL centres are covered by the Rehabilitation of Offenders Act 1974 (Exceptions) Order 1975, employment will be subject to satisfactory clearance from the Criminal Records Bureau (CRB) and other agencies as used by PGL. CRB checks provide PGL with access to a range of different types of information about you, such as relevant information held on the Police National Computer, including any spent or unspent convictions, cautions, reprimands or warnings. Minor, irrelevant misdemeanours are unlikely to affect your application. All information will be treated sensitively and in confidence.

Please give any details on a separate sheet of any of the above that may appear on your CRB disclosure document.

If you have attached a separate sheet, please tick ☐

If you have any questions about your criminal record in relation to this application, please contact the PGL Recruitment Team on 0870 401 4411 in confidence.

BRIEFLY DESCRIBE YOUR PERSONALITY:

WHY DO YOU WANT TO WORK FOR PGL?

HOW DID YOU HEAR ABOUT PGL? PLEASE GIVE NAME OF WEBSITE, NEWSPAPER, MAGAZINE, FRIEND ETC.

➤ ADDITIONAL INFORMATION

Do you require any specific assistance, equipment, support or adjustments to be made to enable you to live on centre and to carry out the position for which you have applied?

☐ Yes ☐ No

If yes, please detail what assistance may be required:

(Use additional sheet if required)

➤ REFERENCES

You **must** provide the name, address and tel/fax number of **three** people who we can contact for a confidential reference.

■ These must ideally be people who you have been in contact with **during the last 2 years** and who can give a reference regarding your suitability, experience and skills for this type of work (e.g. coach, youth leader, former employers/teachers).

■ **We will not accept references from friends, colleagues or neighbours.**

■ We may contact referees **immediately**, so make sure that the addresses are current for the next few weeks (do not give college or school addresses during the holidays).

All job offers are subject to the receipt of satisfactory references. We cannot process your application unless you include 3 referees.

1. NAME

COMPANY

ADDRESS

TEL   FAX

EMAIL

WHAT IS THEIR RELATIONSHIP TO YOU?
EMPLOYER / LECTURER / TEACHER / OTHER (PLEASE STATE):

2. NAME

COMPANY

ADDRESS

TEL   FAX

EMAIL

WHAT IS THEIR RELATIONSHIP TO YOU?
EMPLOYER / LECTURER / TEACHER / OTHER (PLEASE STATE):

3. NAME

COMPANY

ADDRESS

TEL   FAX

EMAIL

WHAT IS THEIR RELATIONSHIP TO YOU?
EMPLOYER / LECTURER / TEACHER / OTHER (PLEASE STATE):

I certify that the information given in connection with this application is true and correct and that if offered employment by PGL, any material changes to the information supplied will be declared.

I have read the data protection section of this form and consent to the use of my personal information for PGL's administration, monitoring or marketing purposes.

Please include photocopies of certificates and driving licence. Ensure you fill out all parts of this form in full, even if you have enclosed other documentation such as a CV.

SIGNED   DATED

Please return to: PGL Recruitment Team, PGL Travel Ltd., Alton Court, Penyard Lane, Ross-on-Wye, Herefordshire, HR9 5GL, UK

www.pgl.co.uk/recruitment   recruitment@pgl.co.uk   00 44 (0) 870 401 44 11

Fig. 9. cont.

Throughout the time leading up to the interview you should still be applying for other jobs, because:

* you might not be offered the job after the interview;
* you might attend the interview and find that the job was not what you expected it to be;
* you might discover another job that you prefer.

Preparing for the interview

Once you are given an interview don't just sit back with a warm glow and presume that you have the job. There will be several other interviewees, and the person who succeeds will be the one who is most impressive at interview. The difference between all of them often comes down to *preparation*.

First, and this is most important, note the time, date and place in your diary, or somewhere where you cannot lose it or forget it.

Secondly, if it gives the name of the interviewer, make sure you know what sex they are and how to pronounce their name. If you are unsure about any of this you should phone their personal secretary and enquire. Don't be embarrassed. Explain that you are confirming your appointment and would like to check on a few facts. You will not be regarded as someone who is unsure or lacking in confidence, but rather somebody who is organised and likes to be thoroughly prepared.

Then, out of courtesy, write to thank them for offering you an interview, and confirm the time and date that you will be attending.

Research counts

Now the work begins that can be the difference between success and failure. If you have applied to a company the chances are that they will have sent you some literature about their operation. Read it thoroughly. Make notes about the things that are big advantages in the job, and also anything that you want to ask questions about. During the interview you will probably have the opportunity to use this information. You will therefore appear to be well prepared and concerned about the company that you are hoping to work for – Big Brownie Points!

If you are preparing to work for a smaller firm that doesn't forward this sort of literature they will be more difficult to research. Nevertheless, you should still try to find as much out about them as possible and the local reference library and internet are good places to start. You can find information on all limited companies through the internet by accessing the Companies House website. The reference library should also carry details of all local limited companies and all back issues of numerous newspapers including the regional daily. You can also use the technique that was suggested in the earlier chapters with regards to finding a job – that of talking to local people. This could be at the library, the local pub, newsagents, garage, anywhere.

The above techniques can also be used if applying to a sports club but extra information can also be gained by the following.

- Checking out performance details and other background information in a specialist sports magazine or local newspaper.

- Seeking out people who have played or worked for this club and talking to them. There should also be plenty of players who have played against them and who can give an alternative opinion.

Making notes

Don't assume that you can remember everything that you find out about this company. Make notes. You may think that you will find out only a small amount of information which will be easily remembered, and this might be true. However, if you find out more than you anticipated some of the earlier data may be forgotten, so write it down. This will also be useful to revise from later and could also be helpful in formulating questions to ask in the interview.

ATTENDING THE INTERVIEW OR SPORTS TRIAL

There are certain things that are of utmost importance when attending an interview or sports trial. Ignore them at your peril.

- Don't be late.
- Don't turn up on the wrong day.
- Do note the location of the interview.

If you are unsure how to get there either check in an A–Z of the area, or go to Google Maps on the internet. Don't presume that you will just be able to drive there using your car's satnav. I know of numerous incidents where this has failed. If still unsure, enquire about the travel directions with the secretary. This could be discussed at your initial contact with them, or it could be asked when confirming your interview. It would also be a good idea to ask about car parking. Many a candidate has been late for an interview, even though they arrived in plenty of time, because they couldn't find a parking spot. There is also a possibility of getting stuck in a one way system or roadworks, so ask about these as well and allow plenty of time.

These enquiries show excellent interview preparation and the secretary is bound to mention this to the boss.

Succeeding at the interview

When you eventually enter the interview a few essential points are worth observing.

1. Be smartly dressed. If you can't make the effort to look good at the interview it will be taken as a sign that you will not make the effort in the job and could also produce shoddy work.

2. Be polite. Even if the interviewer introduces himself as Bill Jones, still call him Mr Jones throughout the interview.

3. Address the interviewer(s) by name. If he hasn't introduced himself, it is a big plus point to say 'Good morning, you must be Mr Jones.'

4. Look interested and confident. When the interviewer talks to you, or you are replying, look them straight in the eye. If you are nervous and look at the floor, or out of the window, this may be taken as a sign of disinterest or that you lack the confidence that they require.

Asking questions

Details of an excellent book *How to Win at Job Hunting*, are given in Chapter 10. This book goes into great detail about the sort of questions you could ask and those that may be asked of you.

Asking questions at the end of the interview shows that you are still interested in the job – but don't overdo it. Remember the interviewers may be on a tight schedule. Only one or two questions are recommended.

A big mistake is to ask questions that have been covered in their literature or during the interview. Interviewers will get the impression that you have been inattentive. If there is something from either that you didn't understand, you can get away with these questions by stating 'there was one thing from the brochure (or interview) that I was unsure of . . .' In this way you have already acknowledged that you know it has already been covered.

Good questions to ask would be about the following.

◆ Training – especially if this is your first job.

◆ Colleagues – who your superiors and subordinates would be.

◆ Responsibilities – what you are responsible for and whether there are any foreseeable problems.

◆ Salary – not recommended, early in the interview, to ask about salary, holidays or hours of work, as these may seem all that you are interested in.

At the end though, if any of these haven't been covered, it is vital to ask these questions.

SUMMARY

◆ Take your time with your application letter – make it neat and formal.

◆ Fill in the application form in black or blue ink – neatly.

◆ Take your time with your CV – type it and don't omit anything.

◆ Keep all your references and testimonials neat and tidy – they are very valuable.

◆ When offered an interview – still apply for other jobs.

◆ Be early for your interview – dress smartly and be polite.

◆ Revise for your interview – make a note of the questions you want to ask.

9

Accepting the Offer and Making Other Arrangements

ACCEPTING THE OFFER

If things have gone to plan you will be reading this section after you have been offered employment. Now you will need to tidy up some loose ends. You can accept the offer verbally, but before signing anything make sure that you have been given a copy of your terms of employment.

Terms of employment

These should include a job description, salary, weekly hours, holiday arrangements, any training necessary for the job, overtime pay and other relevant arrangements. If you are working abroad the arrangements for National Insurance contributions (see later in this chapter) should also be addressed.

If any of this has not been given to you in writing you should ask for this when you verbally agree to take the job. If your job is abroad you should ask your employer whether they take care of visa arrangements, or whether it is your responsibility.

If you have cleared up all the above, the company will probably have a formal contract for you to sign. If, however, they are a smaller company that doesn't issue one of these you may need to write a letter of acceptance (see Figure 10). This is a simple confirmation and a gesture of thanks which may include any

11 Oxford Street
Uptown
Surrey UP2 4YU
Tel: 0198 765432

10 April 201X

Monsieur Didier St Jean
Manager, Hotel Belle Vue
Valmorel
France

Cher Monsieur St Jean,

Thank you for offering me the position of chalet maid at your hotel.

I am very pleased to accept the position and I look forward to working with you in such a beautiful part of France.

One thing we didn't discuss, however, at the interview was my National Insurance contributions. I would be pleased if you could inform me of the arrangments for these.

Yours faithfully,

Michelle Morrison

Michelle Morrison

Fig. 10. Sample letter accepting employment.

further questions that have not been covered above, such as travel arrangements, etc. Make a copy, for yourself, of this letter.

TRAINING FOR THE JOB

If you have accepted employment from private individuals or a small company, it is highly likely that they will expect you to have already trained and qualified for this job. You should already have the experience necessary to execute all of the required tasks of this work. Refer back to Chapter 7 if necessary.

Alternatively, if you are due to work for a big company the majority of them conduct their own training courses so that everybody, even if already qualified, is inducted into their way of doing things. This training period is a good way of meeting your new employers, supervisors and colleagues, and also gives you a chance to get mistakes out of the way before being put into a pressure situation where it could be more embarrassing and expensive.

If you have been offered a job that doesn't give training and you are not confident enough to go straight into it, or maybe you are qualified but have had a long break from this type of work, then it may be a good idea to look for some relevant voluntary work before starting with your new employer.

COLLECTING THE NECESSARY DOCUMENTS

If you are British, and working in Britain, you can skip this section. If you plan to work abroad you will need some, or all, of the following documents before you can work legally in a foreign country.

Passport

Obtaining a passport for a British Citizen is fairly

straightforward as long as you apply in plenty of time. This process has been made even easier with the opening of the Identity and Passport Service (IPS) on 1 April 2006, so that the majority of this transaction can be conducted online over the internet, simply type in www.ips.gov.uk. The IPS recommend that you apply at least one month before needing to use this passport, if this is your first one. You can fast-track this process, down to as little as one week, but it will be more expensive and may involve travelling to your nearest passport office and waiting in a queue.

Passport Offices are located in Belfast, Durham, Glasgow, London, Liverpool, Newport and Peterborough. Enquiries can be made, and application forms obtained, from most main post offices, many travel agents, or by telephoning 0800 222 0000, or logging on to the above website.

Always keep your passport safe and make a note of its number and place of issue in case of difficulties or, more particularly, in case it is stolen or you lose it. It is also a good idea to make a photocopy, or a scan onto your computer's hard disk, of its main page at home before departure.

Obtaining visas and work permits

If your employment is in the European Union there is no need to obtain a visa or work permit before starting work. For many other countries outside the EU you will need both to be able to work there. Obtaining these can be a very lengthy and difficult process, so start negotiating these as soon as possible after being offered the job.

If you are lucky your employer may take care of this for you. If you are not, however, you need to contact the consular section of the appropriate embassy as soon as possible. These are generally found in London and are quite easy to trace through *Yellow Pages* or your local library or, of course, through the internet.

The consul of this embassy will then advise you of the procedure, which normally requires you to supply the following:

+ your passport;
+ your birth certificate;
+ a medical certificate;
+ your educational qualifications;
+ two passport-size photographs;
+ your marriage certificate (if this is relevant).

TAKING MEDICAL PRECAUTIONS

If you are taking up a job in Britain you can miss this section, however if you are going to work abroad the following should be carefully noted, especially if you are going to work in a remote region.

Over recent years the health care in many countries has become as good as, or better than, that in Britain, but it can be costly to obtain. Not many have a 'free' health service like ours, so a few precautions are well worth taking before commencing employment abroad.

1. First, make sure you are fit for the job. If it is going to be strenuous, work out before you go. Also ensure you are medically fit.

2. Have all your check-ups before you go – dental, medical and optical.

3. If you wear glasses take a spare pair. If you use any other appliances, and a spare is out of the question, make sure you have the appliance serviced. In the case of battery driven aids, such as for hearing, make sure you take a spare battery.

4. Have a course of vaccinations. These can take some time so check with your GP early. Typhoid, for example, requires two injections, one month apart. You can normally find out from the embassy which vaccinations are required, but the Department of Health produces a leaflet on this which you can obtain from your local surgery. They also have extensive information on their website www.dh.gov.uk.

5. Take with you any medication that you would normally use in Britain. If on an extended visit, make sure you have enough to cover its duration. Also take a first aid box that might include as well as the usual plasters, antiseptic cream and paracetamol, things like:
   insect repellent;
   anti-malaria pills;
   travel sickness tablets;
   anti-diarrhoea medication.
   And don't forget (hopefully you'll need) suntan lotion.

6. If you are working in the European Economic Area (EEA) obtain a European Health Insurance Card (EHIC) which entitles you to reduced cost, sometimes free, medical treatment. This replaces the old E111 certificate.

The EEA consists of the European Union (EU) countries plus Iceland, Liechtenstein and Norway. Switzerland applies the EHIC arrangements through an agreement with the EU. It must be stressed, however, that this provides for *emergency* treatment only. If you need to stay in hospital after the initial treatment you will have to pay for it, so it is well worth taking out insurance. This will normally be in an all-in policy which also covers you for loss of equipment, baggage, money passports, etc.

It must also be noted that you may have to pay for this emergency treatment whilst abroad and then reclaim the costs when you return to the UK. So take a credit card with you with an adequate upper credit limit available. In most cases you will not be able to reclaim the full amount, but you might be able to claim for the difference through your insurers. Check before taking out the policy.

COMPLYING WITH NATIONAL INSURANCE REQUIREMENTS

You need to know, before you leave, what the arrangements are for your National Insurance contributions. Your new employer should be able to tell you this. However, if they are not sure then they, or you, can obtain advice and information from your local Department of Work and Pensions (DWP) Office, or by accessing the website www.dwp.gov.uk. This is extremely important as these arrangements will ensure that you are covered, even if working abroad, for losing your job, falling ill and numerous other benefits.

TRAVELLING THERE

If you are working in the UK you should be able to plan your travel arrangements by discussing them with family and friends, or by contacting your local bus, train or flight operator.

If you are working abroad you might need to make special arrangements, but usually your employer will help you with these and the cost is regularly included as part of your contract.

If you do have to make your own arrangements, however, there are a few useful points to remember.

♦ Make your arrangements early. If you leave it late you might not be able to find discounted travel. Worse still, you might not be able to get there at all.

♦ Look for the most convenient and suitable way of getting to your destination – the cheapest is not always the best.

♦ Arrange travel insurance that covers you for cancellations, delays, loss of luggage, etc. Take advice from a travel agent or insurance broker if unsure. You can find a multitude of these by conducting a search on the internet.

SUMMARY

♦ Write a letter of acceptance. Use it as a chance to enquire about matters that you are not clear about – especially terms of employment.

♦ Train or prepare yourself for the job.

♦ Make early arrangements for passports, visas and work permits.

♦ Take out insurance. Make sure it covers everything.

♦ Ensure you are physically fit – get medical, optical and dental check-ups.

♦ Take a first aid case.

♦ Make travel arrangements early.

10
Useful Contact Information

I n the last edition of this book the full postal address of most companies was given, but since then a minor revolution has occurred, and now many companies only give their internet address as this is their preferred mode of contact.

COMPANY INFORMATION

Airtours plc. (Now part of the Thomas Cook group)

Backroads, 801 Cedar Street, Berkeley, California 94710-1800.
www.backroads.com

BUNAC, 16 Bowling Green Lane, London EC1R 0QH.
Tel: 020 7251 3472. www.bunac.org.uk

Camp America, 37a Queens Gate, London SW7 5H.
Tel: 011 4420 75817373. www.campamerica.co.uk

Canvas Holidays, Tle: 0845 2680827. www.canvasholidays.co.uk

ClubMed, www.clubmedjobs.com

Cross-Cultural Solutions, Tower Point, 44 North Road,
Brighton BN1 1YR. Tel: 0845 458 2781/2.
www.crossculturalsolutions.org

Crystal Holidays, Kings Place, Wood Street, Kington-upon-
Thames, Surey KT1 1JY. www.crystalholidays.co.uk

Eurocamp, Hartford Manor, Greenbank Lane, Northwich
CW8 1HW. Tel: 01606 787522. www.eurocamp.co.uk

European Waterways, 35 Wharf Road, Wraysbury, Middlesex
TW19 5JQ. Tel: (01784) 482439. www.gobarging.com

Halsbury Travel, 35 Churchill Park,Colwick Business Est, Notts
NG4 2HF. Tel: (0115) 940 4303. www.halsbury.com

Ian Mearns Holidays, Tannery Yard, Witney St, Burford Oxon

OX18 4DP. Tel: (01993) 822655. www.ianmearnsholidays.co.uk
Keycamp, Hartford Manor, Greenbank Lane, Northwich
   CW8 1HW. Tel: 0844 406 0311. www.holidaybreakjobs.com
Mark Warner Ltd, 20 Kensington Church Street, London W8
   4EP. Tel: 0817 033955. www.markwarner-recruitment.co.uk
PGL, Alton Court, Penyard Lane, Ross-on-Wye, Hereford
   HR9 5GL. Tel: 0844 3710101. www.pgl.co.uk
Ramblers Holidays, Lemsford Mill, Welwyn Garden City
   AL8 7TR. Tel: (01707) 331133. www.ramblersholidays.co.uk
Sunsail, The Port House, Port Solent, Portsmouth PO6 4TH.
   Tel: (023) 9222 2329. www.sunsail.co.uk
TUI Travel Recruitment, Jetset House, Lowfield Heath, Crawley
   RH11 0PQ. Tel: 0800 169 5692. www.firstchoice4jobs.co.uk
VSO Voluntary Service Overseas, 37a Carlton Drive, Putney,
   London SW15 2BS. Tel: (020) 8780 7500. www.vso.org.uk

BOOK INFORMATION

Listed below is the information on numerous books that will be useful in finding employment in sport. Most are available from the job section of public libraries, but if you run into difficulties it should be possible, with the information given, to order them from major book stores.

A Guide to Jobs and Qualifications in Sport And Recreation,
   John Potter/ILAM (John Potter Publications).
A Guide to Professional Sport, Various (The Institute of
   Professional Sport).
A Year Off . . . or A Year, Suzanne Straw (Hobson/CRAC).
Careers in Sport, Compendium (The Sports Council).
Careers in Sport, Louise Fyfe (Kogan Page).
Careers in Teaching, Ewan McLeish (Trotman).
Careers in the Travel Industry, C. Chester (Kogan Page).
Cruise Ship Job Guide, John Kenning (Harper Publications).

Getting A Job Abroad, Roger Jones (How To Books).

Getting A Job In Travel And Tourism, Mark Hempshell (How To Books).

How to Find Temporary Work Abroad, Nick Vandome (How To Books).

How to Travel Round the World, Nick Vandome (How To Books).

How to Win at Job Hunting, Ian Maitland (Century Business).

International Directory Of Voluntary Work, Editor David Woodworth (Vacation Work Pubs.).

Live and Work in France/Germany/Italy/Spain and Portugal, Vacation Work Publications.

Soccer Coach USA, Delta Publications.

Sports Scholarships and College Programs in the USA, Editor Ron Walker (Petersons).

Summer Jobs Abroad, Editor David Woodworth (Vacation Work Pubs.).

Summer Jobs USA, Peterson's Guides (Vacation Work Pubs.).

Taking A Year Off, Val Butcher (Trotman).

USA College Soccer, Delta Publications.

Voluntary Agencies Directory, Various (NCVO Publications).

Volunteer Work, Central Bureau for Educational Visits and Exchanges.

Working Abroad, Susan Griffith (Kogan Page).

Working in Leisure, COIC (COIC).

Working in Ski Resorts, V. Pybus and C. James (Vacation Work Pubs.).

Yacht Crew Jobs, Delta Publications.

MAGAZINE AND NEWSPAPER INFORMATION

Ace Tennis Magazine, 20 Upper Ground, London SE1 9PD.

Aikido Journal, 452 E. Silverado Ranch Blvd. #361 Las Vegas, NV 89183. Tel: 702-837-7657 www.aikidojournal.com

Anglers Mail, IPC Magazines, 10 Southwark Street, London SE1 0SU.

Angling Times, EMAP Publishing, Greater London House,
 Hampstead Road, London NW1 7EJ.

Athletics Weekly, P.O. Box 614, Farnham, Surrey GU9 1PE.

Bicycling, Tel: USA 800 6662806. www.bicycling.com

Boat Fishing, www.warnersgroup.co.uk

Boat International, P.O. Box 326, Sittingbourne, Kent ME9 8PX.

Camping Magazine, www.warnersgroup.co.uk

Country Walking, Media House, Lynch Wood, Peterborough
 PE2 6EA.

Combat Magazine, Unit 20, Maybrook Business Park, Minworth,
 Sutton Coldfield B7 1BE. Tel: 0121 351 6930.
 www.combatmag.co.uk

Cycling Plus, Future Publishing, 30 Monmouth Street, Bath
 BA1 2BW.

Cycle Sport, IPC Magazines, 10 Southwark Street, London
 SE1 0SU.

Cycling Active, IPC Magazines, 10 Southwark Street, London
 SE1 0SU.

Cycling Weekly, IPC Magazines, 10 Southwark Street, London
 SE1 0SU.

Cycling World, Andrew House, 2a Granville Rd., Sidcup
 DA14 4BN.

Equestrian Times, International Equestrian News Network,
 P.O. Box 227, Marshfield Hills, MA 02051 USA.
 Tel: + 1 781 834 7137.

Eventing, IPC Magazines, 10 Southwark Street, London
 SE1 0SU.

Footballers World, Newton Wells, 57 High Street, Hampton
 TW12 2SX.

FourFourTwo, P.O.Box 326, Sittingbourne, Kent ME9 8FA.
 Tel: 08456 777811. www.fourfourtwo.magazine.uk

Golf Monthly, IPC Magazines, 10 Southwark Street, London
 SE1 0SU.

Golf Week, 1500 Park Center Drive, Orlando, FL 32835, USA.

Golf World, Media House, Lynch Wood, Peterborough PE2 6EA.

The Golfer Magazine, Fairway Media Ltd., Cross Street Mill, Leek ST13 6BL.

The Good Ski Guide, 91 High Street, Esher, Surrey KT10 9QD.

Health & Fitness, Dennis Publishing, 30 Cleveland Street, London W1T 4JD. Tel: 0844 8440081.

Hockey News (Ice Hockey), 25 Sheppard Ave., Suite 100, Toronto, ON M2N 6S7. Tel: 1-888-361-9768. www.thehockeynews.com

Horse, IPC Magazines, 10 Southwark Street, London SE1 0SU.

Horse & Hound, IPC Magazines, 10 Southwark Street, London SE1 0SU.

Lakeland Walker, www.warnersgroup.co.uk

Match!, Media House, Lynch Wood, Peterborough PE2 6EA.

Men's Fitness, Dennis Publishing, 30 Cleveland Street, London W1T 4JD. Tel: 0844 8440081.

Motor Boat & Yachting, IPC Magazines, 10 Southwark Street, London SE1 0SU.

Mountain Bike, Tel: USA 800 6662806. www.mountainbike.com

Mountain Bike Rider, IPC Magazines, 10 Southwark Street, London SE1 0SU.

Mountain Biking UK, Future Publishing, 30 Monmouth Street, Bath BA1 2BW.

National Club Golfer, 18–22 Market Street, Cleckheaton, BD19 5AJ. Tel: 01274 851 323.

Overseas Jobs Express.co.uk Newspaper and site currently under reconstruction www.overseasjobsexpress.co.uk

ProCycling, Future Publishing, 30 Monmouth Street, Bath BA1 2BW.

Rugby World, IPC Magazines, 10 Southwark Street, London SE1 0SU.

Runner's World, Tel: USA 800 666 2828. www.runnersworld.com

Running Times, Tel: USA 800 666 4735. www.runningtimes.com

The Shooting Gazette, IPC Magazines, 10 Southwark Street, London SE1 0SU.

Sport Diver, Prospect House, Surrey CR9 2TA. Tel: 020 8686 2599.

Sport Mountain Biker International Magazine, IPC Media Ltd, Croydon, Surrey CR9 2TA. Tel: 020 8686 2599.

Sporting Gun, IPC Magazines, 10 Southwark Street, London SE1 0SU.

Swimming Times, 21 Granby Street, Loughborough LE11 3DU. Tel: 01509 632233.

Today's Golfer, Media House, Lynch Wood, Peterborough PE2 6EA.

Total Fitness Magazine (now only website). www.facebook.com/TotalFitnessMagazine#!

Triathlon Plus, Future Publishing, 30 Monmouth Street, Bath BA1 2BW.

Waterski, 460 North Orlando Ave., Suite 200, Winter Park FL32789, USA.

Windsurf Magazine, The Blue Barns, Thew Lane, Wootton, Woodstock OX20 1HA. www.windsurf.co.uk

Working Abroad Magazine, www.workingabroadmagazine.com

World Soccer, IPC Magazines, 10 Southwark Street, London SE1 0SU.

Yachting Monthly, IPC Magazines, 10 Southwark Street, London SE1 0SU.

Yachting World, IPC Magazines, 10 Southwark Street, London SE1 0SU.

Your Horse, Media House, Lynch Wood, Peterborough PE2 6EA.

WEBSITES THAT CONTAIN A SPORTS EMPLOYMENT CATEGORY

There is a multitude of websites on the internet advertising employment opportunities. Listed below are just a small number of them that have recently advertised work with a sporting bias.

If you want to work abroad a very useful website that you should access is www.workingabroadmagazine.com It details employment available as tour guides, teaching English, on cruise ships, in summer camps, and much, much more.

Also try the websites listed below, which may also contain different jobs not listed in the above site.

sunsail.co.uk	ukelife.com	ultraforce.co.uk
uksport.gov.uk	golfergirlcareers.com	tennis.com
goodskiguide.com	skiconnection.co.uk	ski-jobs.co.uk
skiingonashoestring.com	waterskimag.com	swimtime.org
jobsite.co.uk	myjobsearch.com	jobrapido.com
indeed.com	jobs24.co.uk	reed.co.uk
CV-library.co.uk	gumtree.com	globalchoices.co.uk
uksport.gov.uk	fish4jobs.co.uk	leisurejobs.com
totaljobs.com		

WORK NOT DIRECTLY CONNECTED TO YOUR SPORT

There are also many overseas opportunities advertised in the following journals that are available from most leading newsagents or through your local reference library.

Entertainment – *Melody Maker, Record Mirror, The Stage, The White Book.*

General – *The Working Traveller, Overseas Jobs Express, JobSearch, The Lady, Nursing Times.*

Careers Europe is the UK National Resource Centre for International Careers Information. It provides resources to careers services, Connexions services and other information and advisory services throughout the UK (www.careerseurope.co.uk).

Glossary

Abseiling A rock-climbing term for descending a rock face, or any other near vertical structure, using only a rope and possibly a harness. The Royal Marines and SAS are often seen on the TV doing this at great speed.

Accessing A term often used in computing to denote entering a computer program. Most commonly used for gaining entry to internet websites.

Activity holidays Holidays during which the holidaymakers take part in one or more activities such as golf, tennis, skiing, windsurfing, etc.

Assistantship See Graduate Assistantship.

BASI British Association of Snowsports Instructors.

BMX The full title is bicycle moto cross. Participants race against each other on specially adapted bikes over rough terrain.

BTEC The abbreviation of Business and Technician Education Council. A body that administers many sports related courses and examinations. See Chapter 7.

BUCS British Universities and Colleges Sport.

BUNAC The abbreviation of British Universities North America Club. They have been arranging employment at summer camps in the USA and Canada since 1962. They now also arrange work in other countries like Australia, Ghana, Jamaica, Malta, New Zealand, Spain and South Africa, but the latter is generally of the non-sports type.

Bursary See also scholarships. Bursaries tend to be small grants to students whereas scholarships are much bigger and can be awarded to cover a longer period of time.

Camp counselling A job, mainly in summer camps, that entails looking after the needs of the younger participants on the course.

CCPR The Central Council for Physical Recreation. One of the oldest established sporting bodies in the United Kingdom.

City and Guilds Short for the City and Guilds London Institute. A body that administers many sports related courses and examinations. See Chapter 7.

CV The abbreviation of curriculum vitae. Literally meaning History of Life, also called a 'resumé', mainly in the United States, this is simply a record of your education, employment and interests. Generally asked for by prospective employers prior to drawing up a shortlist for interview.

Cybercafé A commercial enterprise found on the high streets of many major cities that offers clients access to the internet, for a small fee. See also Internet café.

Dude ranches A thriving, vibrant holiday retreat in North America that gives guests a taste of the old Wild West (without too much discomfort).

Embassy In the UK most embassies are normally found in London, and are the British headquarters of friendly overseas countries. You need to contact them to arrange visas and work permits.

Gap year See Year out.

Graduate A person who holds a degree from a university or college.

Graduate Assistantship Normally abbreviated just to Assistantship. These are university places given to graduates who normally receive a grant to cover the cost of their studies for a higher level degree course in return for some teaching or coaching. Sports Assistantships are usually found in the USA.

ILAM An abbreviation of the Institute of Leisure and Amenity Management who administer their own internal examinations. See Chapter 7.

Internet The internet was developed in 1969 as a means of passing information from one computer to another. It has been referred to as 'the information superhighway' and it is a very fast way of accessing all kinds of information from all around the world.

Internet café A commercial enterprise found on the high streets of many major cities that offers clients access to the internet, for a small fee. See also Cybercafé.

Leisure company One of a growing number of companies set up to cater for holidaymakers' needs. They normally arrange things from flights, accommodation and currency, to sports courses and competitions.

NVQ Abbreviation of the National Vocational Qualification. This is awarded by many schools and colleges around Britain and many courses are sports based. More details in Chapter 7.

Passport A formal document issued by the Passport Office (see Chapter 9). This entitles you to leave Britain for another country. There are seven Passport Offices around Britain and application can now be made online.

PFA The Professional Footballers' Association.

Prize money Money gained by winning or being placed in a tournament. A precarious way of earning a living. If you don't win you don't eat.

Pro Abbreviated form of Professional (see below).

Professional In sporting terms, a person who makes a living out of sport.

Professional (golf) A golf pro makes a living out of coaching, organising tournaments and running a golf shop.

Professional (tournament) A golf tournament pro plays for a living and makes money out of being placed highly in tournaments, as well as receiving sponsorship and advertising revenue.

PTI Abbreviation of Physical Training Instructor. A position held in the Armed Forces (see Chapter 2).

References A record of your employment with an employer who normally sends them, on request, to a prospective employer.

Rep Abbreviated form of representative. This is a person who represents a holiday company or similar organisation and is employed to look after their clients.

Resumé See CV.

Scholarship Scholarships are grants that are often awarded to students who universities and colleges are keen to enrol. They vary in size from a couple of hundred pounds to thousands. See Chapter 3 for more details.

Semi-Pro A person who makes money through sport, but not enough to live on, so has another job to boost earnings.

Shortlist A list of candidates for a job that has been reduced from all applications, and normally the ones that have been selected for interview.

The Six Nations Championship An international Rugby Union tournament between England, France, Ireland, Italy, Scotland and Wales.

Sponsorship Funding given to sportspeople, mainly by commercial organisations, in return for the promotion of their product.

Sport England The National Governing Body for sport in England. See Chapter 6.

Sport Scotland The National Governing Body for sport in Scotland. See Chapter 6.

Sports Council The old name for the National Governing Body for sport in the UK. Replaced by Sports Councils for the individual countries: England, Ireland, Scotland and Wales.

Sports Council for Northern Ireland The National Governing Body for sport in Northern Ireland. See Chapter 6.

Sports Council for Wales The National Governing Body for sport in Wales. See Chapter 6.

Summer camp Originally an American concept but now growing in popularity around the world. These holiday camps are set up to usefully occupy schoolchildren during their long summer break. Courses range from arts and crafts to numerous sports.

Terms of employment A document that should be supplied by an employer detailing the working practice and conditions for new employees.

Visa Many countries outside the European Union require visitors to obtain an entry permit, or visa, for their country. These are normally acquired, *before* travelling, from their embassy, to allow immigration.

Voluntary work Historically this was unpaid work for a charitable organisation. Now some of this work carries a small salary – normally enough to cover all incurred expenses plus a little pocket money. Flights, accommodation, food and sometimes clothes are covered. See Chapter 4 for more details.

VSO An abbreviation of Voluntary Service Overseas. A long-established reputable aid agency. See Chapter 4 for more details.

Women's Sport & Fitness Federation (WSFF) (previously WSF).

Work permit Many countries outside the European Union require visitors to hold a work permit for their country before being allowed through immigration. These are normally acquired, *before* travelling, from their embassy.

Year out Taking a 'year out' or a 'gap year' is the term commonly used by students who either take a break from studies before going to university, or part way through their course, or after finishing but before taking up their chosen career.

Notes

1. The Central Council for Physical Recreation (CCPR).
2. The *Sunday Times* 'Rich List' 2010 edited by Philip Beresford.
3. *Futebol Finance* by Kaitlin Madden, CareerBuilder.com.
4. The Professional Footballers' Association: www.gimmefootball.com.
5. Myjobsearch.com.
6. Women's Sport and Fitness Foundation: www.wsff.org.uk.
7. Jacqui Oatley, BBC Sport Football, 15 November 2007.
8. Workforce and Skills Summary: SkillsActive.com, 2009.

Index

Some other titles from How To Books

HOW TO SUCCEED AT INTERVIEWS
DR ROB YEUNG

'Yeung's book is clearly written and to the point.... to be interviewed without having read it is an opportunity missed.' – *Sunday Times*

'... the type of book that one may not wish to share with others who are job seeking in competition with oneself.' – S. Lewis, Coventry

'An invaluable source of information, tests and assessment centres.' – Jonathan Turpin, Chief Executive, fish4job.co.uk

'... packed with useful observations and tips for the job seekers of all ages.' – Roddy Gow, Chairman, Odgers, Ray and Berndtson

'This is an excellent book; good value buy it!' – V. Tilbury, Cranfield University

The new edition of this best-selling book tells you how to:

◆ Give impressive answers to over 200 interview questions
◆ Deal with interview nerves and project total confidence
◆ Pass psychometric tests, competency-based questions, and assessment centres
◆ Avoid the traps that interviewers lay for unwary job seekers
◆ Turn every interview question to your advantage

Business psychologist Dr Rob Yeung trains interviewers and designs assessment centres. Appearing regularly on television he has also presented BBC TV's *How To Get Your Dream Job*.

ISBN 978-1-84528-442-8

WHY SHOULD I WORK FOR YOU?
How to find the job that's right for you – *and* get the offer
KEITH POTTS AND JASON DEIGN

Packed with tips, exercises and case studies, this book will give you all you need to create a 'you-shaped job' and set the course for a better life. Discover: the four things you need to get any job; a unique way of working out which job you should be doing; how to avoid pitfalls in job hunting and interviews; and how to create a life-long plan that will help you enjoy a happy and fulfilling career for the rest of your working days.

ISBN 978-1-84528-347-6

HOW TO PASS THAT JOB INTERVIEW
JULIE-ANN AMOS

This book will give you the confidence to succeed at any interview.

'A welcome addition to any careers library... succeeds in its aim of giving people the confidence to do well at an interview. ... a welcome addition to any careers library.' – Newscheck

ISBN 978-1-84528-426-8

HOW TO WRITE AN IMPRESSIVE CV & COVER LETTER
A comprehensive guide for the UK job seeker
TRACEY WHITMORE

Includes a CD with templates and real-life examples

'I like this book as all of the templates on the attached CD are free. Overall one of the most fully comprehensive 'how to' prepare to get the job books I have seen in a long time.' – www.student-express.com

'The book and CD are packed with practical examples of CVs and cover letters that we worked in real-life.' – Orange Standard

ISBN 978-1-84528-365-0

HANDLING TOUGH JOB INTERVIEWS
Be prepared, perform well, get the job
JULIE-ANN AMOS

'The book gives a wealth of sound advice, including good hints on how to make the right impression, the best questions to ask, how to approach negotiating a salary, taking a psychometric test and how you should treat a regular interview differently from one with a recruitment agency or a head-hunter.' – SESAME, Open University magazine

ISBN 978-1-84528-358-2

How To Books are available through all good bookshops, or you can order direct from us through Grantham Book Services.

Tel: +44 (0)1476 541080
Fax: +44 (0)1476 541061
Email: orders@gbs.tbs-ltd.co.uk

Or via our website
www.howtobooks.co.uk

To order via any of these methods please quote the title(s) of the book(s) and your credit card number together with its expiry date.

For further information about our books and catalogue, please contact:

How To Books
Spring Hill House
Spring Hill Road
Begbroke
Oxford OX5 1RX

Visit our web site at
www.howtobooks.co.uk

Or you can contact us by email at info@howtobooks.co.uk